Game On!

GAME ON!

FROM PONG TO OBLIVION

THE 50 GREATEST VIDEO GAMES OF ALL TIME

Simon Byron Ste Curran David McCarthy

headline

First published in 2006 by
HEADLINE PUBLISHING GROUP

1

Cataloguing in Publication Data is available from the British Library

0 7553 1570 7 (ISBN-10)
978 0 7553 1570 3 (ISBN-13)

Designed by Dan Newman @ Perfect Bound Ltd

Printed and bound by Rotolito Lombarda, Italy.

Headline's policy is to use papers that are natural, renewable and recyclable products and made
from wood grown in sustainable forests. The logging and manufacturing processes are expected to
conform to the environmental regulations of the country of origin.

Headline Publishing Group
A division of Hodder Headline
338 Euston Road
London NW1 3BH

www.headline.co.uk
www.hodderheadline.com

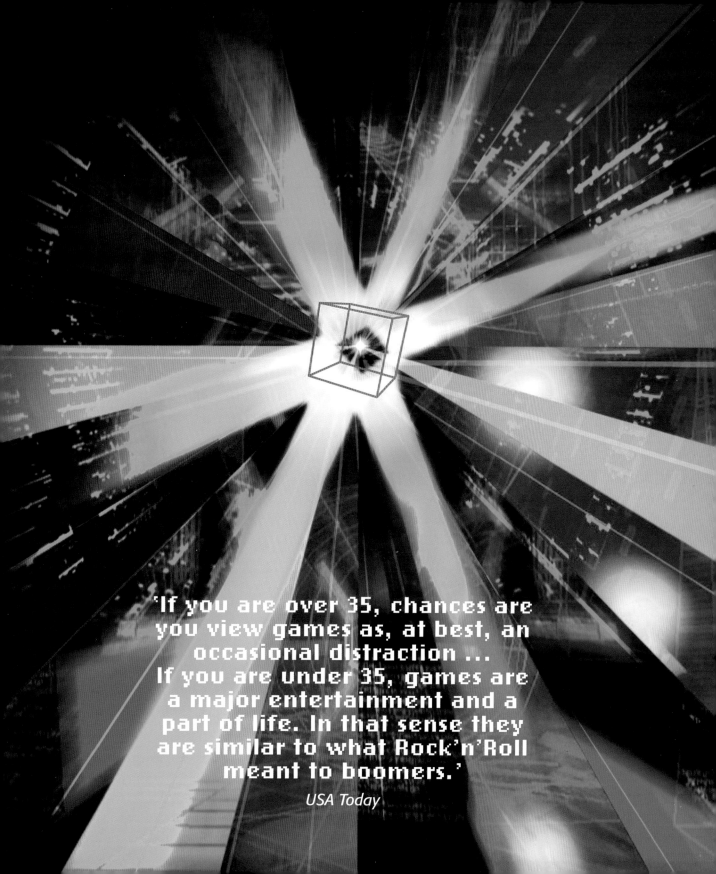

'If you are over 35, chances are you view games as, at best, an occasional distraction ...
If you are under 35, games are a major entertainment and a part of life. In that sense they are similar to what Rock'n'Roll meant to boomers.'

USA Today

Contents

Introduction	8
Advance Wars™: Dual Strike	12
Animal Crossing™: Wild World	16
Asteroids	20
Bangai-O	22
Battlefield 1942™	28
Broken Sword: The Shadow of the Templars	32
Call of Duty 2	38
Command & Conquer™	44
Dance Dance Revolution	48
Dead or Alive 4	52
The Elder Scrolls® IV: Oblivion™	58
°Elite	64
EyeToy®: Play	66
FINAL FANTASY VII	68
F-Zero™ GX	76
GoldenEye 007™	80
Grand Theft Auto III	84
Gran Turismo 4	90
Guitar Hero	94
Half-Life	98
Halo: Combat Evolved	104
Ico™	112
Jak and Daxter: The Precursor Legacy™	118
Jet Set Radio Future	122
The Legend of Zelda™: Ocarina of Time™	126
Lumines	134

Madden NFL 06 136

Mario Kart™ DS 140

Metal Gear Solid 146

OutRun 154

Pac-Man™ 156

Pokémon™ Ruby/Sapphire 158

Pong 164

Pro Evolution Soccer 5 166

Resident Evil™ 4 172

Rez 180

Ridge Racer™ 184

Sid Meier's Civilization II 188

The Sims™ 192

Soulcalibur™ II 198

Space Invaders 204

Street Fighter™ II 208

Super Mario™ 64 214

Super Monkey Ball 222

Tetris™ 226

Tomb Raider 228

Tony Hawk's Pro Skater 3 236

Virtua Tennis 240

Wario Ware™ Inc.: Minigame Mania 244

World of Warcraft 246

Permissions 254

Acknowledgements 256

Introduction

Before you start: it wasn't easy.

Sure, it *sounds* easy, but deciding on the fifty greatest games of all time is as simple as picking the fifty greatest experiences ever, trying to decide if tasting a strawberry is better or worse than skydiving. It's good that gaming's so diverse, that there are adventures for everyone, but there's such a contrast of experiences across the medium. Genres are often impossible to directly compare. Trust us, we've thought about this a lot. We've had to play a lot of games. We know that sounds tough, but we're very brave.

The only solution? To create a book that makes sure it represents that diversity. So that's why this isn't a linear, straightforward top fifty but a patchwork tapestry of videogame brilliance, picking out the fifty highest points from across gaming's beautiful spectrum. The majority of videogaming genres are here, not just the media mainland like shooting and driving – the games that represent what people think games are – but the outlying islands too, like Sony's beautiful *Ico* and Sega's sugar-sweet *Super Monkey Ball*.

Because of this ludicrous, wonderful variation, gaming is the most exciting place to be right now, and those who haven't tried it are missing the experience of their three lives, no continues. Gaming is interactive, it tells stories, it can be wholly abstract, it is bright and dark and fast and slow. It has the capacity to be as touching as it is thrilling, as beautiful as it is horrifying, and it can show as much as grace and elegance as can demonstrate impact and destruction. And you are always in charge, and we have no doubt that someday it will rule the world, someday everyone will play, and someday you'll be able to tell your kids, your grandkids, your great-great-great grand-kids through a hologram reconstruction of yourself inside the PlayStation® XXV: I was there first. I played in those early fictional lands, and I knew how brilliant they were, are, and will be.

That's what this book is meant to be: a travel guide to interactive digital culture, picking out fifty destinations that would-be explorers simply have to visit. The chances are that you'll see many places you've already seen, games you remember from yesterday, last month, last year, a decade ago. We'll help you remember why they were so special, and why you should take the time to pay them another visit. But the chapters on worlds you haven't been to yet; hopefully they'll whet your appetite for another holiday.

And we expect the final list will get you thinking, too. It took long enough to come up with a top fifty that satisfied the three of us, let alone one to placate our countless millions of readers. Even the terms were confusing. Should a list like this include games that kickstarted a genre, or games that defined it? What about games whose sequels improved on their already excellent template? Could the simple graphics and gameplay in old games really stand up to today's high expectations? Do recently released games simply seem better because they're fresher in our memories?

There are no easy answers to any of those questions, so perhaps it's worth us running over the answers we came up with. The first – should we take the first, or the best, in a particular genre – was maybe the most difficult. The answer was to avoid the question and to do both, a cheat code so neat it should come written in the handbooks of all prospective authors. So, some of the titles here justify their places by being classic titles that invented new ways of playing; glimpses of history that everyone should play, games whose retro dynamics still stand up even in the hands of the demanding expectations of today's gamers. Others win their place having forged reputations in the fire of the modern marketplace, despite hundreds of similar (but measurably inferior) experiences all clamouring for attention.

In the specific case that a series warrants a place in the top 50, we've chosen what we feel to be the standout title in that franchise in terms of both brilliance and accessibility – but we've also tried to provide some illumination of the series of a whole, both in the words and the selec- tion of screenshots used. In the case of the *Soul* series, for example, we've selected *Soulcalibur II*, p because it's still currently available to purchase a and partially because, although it lacked the parad impact of the original *SoulCalibur*, it polishes and every aspect of that game without the potential ov plication of creating characters introduced by th game in the series. Clear? Good, so let's move on.

Can simple graphics and gameplay really st today? As mentioned earlier, the gameplay certai While the minimalist and abstract visual side of like *Pong* might not quite cut it next to the comple dour of games like *Oblivion*, the simplistic nature gameplay can actually be a breath of fresh air. don't have to worry about a wealth of options, a very clear objective, and the elementary control them free to concentrate on that: avoid missing high score, indeed.

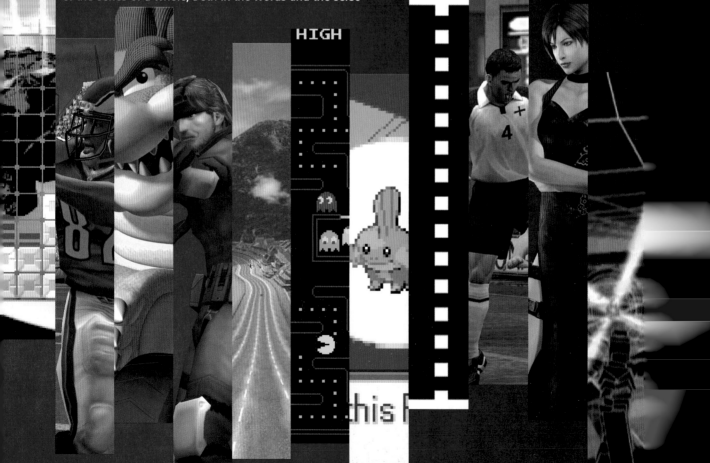

And finally, yes, selections of games like this often tend to skew towards the vivid, crisp, bewitching splendour of more recent memories, overlooking the past in favour of the present. Of course, it's equally important not to go too far in the other direction, those rose-tinted screen overlays can be just as dangerous when it comes to regarding old games. But we've tried to keep a sense of historical perspective throughout, and if the modern games we've picked fail to stand the test of time as well as the older ones have; well, there's always *Game On 2007*.

Flippancy aside, it's important to remember that lists almost always create more debate than they resolve. Accepting that, we have tried to make sure that one thing remains constant throughout ours. There may be games here you don't like, but each and every title here has a passionate, fervent die-hard fanbase who'll fight for its inclusion in the top 50 every bit as much as you'll fight to exclude it.

Because gaming has something for everyone, and if every game in here was for you then the world would be so dull. There are games for girls and games for boys, games for the young and games for the old, games for five minutes and games for five months. There are games here for people who count gaming as their primary interest, and there are games for people who've never picked up a joypad before. Diversity, see? That's why videogaming is the the most exciting creative medium in the world right now, and why writing this book was a joy. Most of the time.

Enjoy the arguments, and cherish our differences. Personal preference will always come into play in lists of the best things ever – a strawberry is much, much better than skydiving. These are our fifty greatest games. There are many other great games we love that didn't quite make it. We leave it as an exercise to the reader to work out what they were. Good luck, and game on.

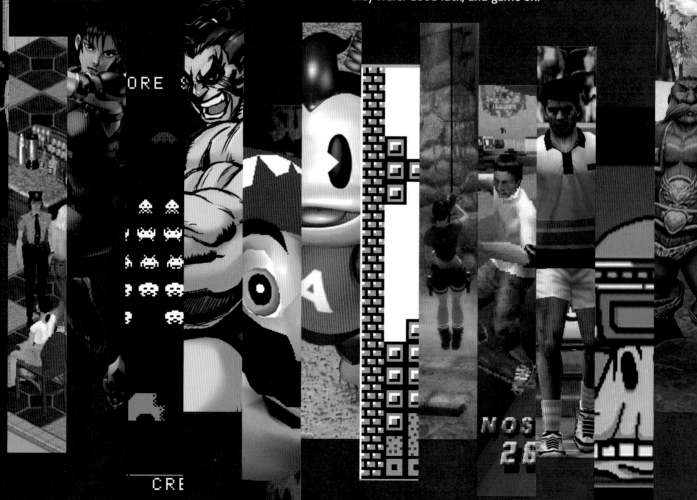

Advance Wars™ : Dual Strike

Publisher: Nintendo
Developer: Intelligent Systems
Format: Nintendo DS
Released: 2005

The setup doesn't really make sense. Nintendo publish games centred around things that are fun and things that look fun, about bright colours, green hills, blue skies and cute characters. War isn't fun, and turn-based war games are pretty much the opposite of all those things. So what happens when Nintendo's development friends EAD make a game about war? They turn out one of the greatest games ever, of course.

Advance Wars: Dual Strike is a turn-based strategy game. That means that it plays out step by step, turn by turn, moves being made one at a time. Players begin with a certain number of military units at their disposal, tiny little pieces like counters in a board game. They move them across the board and try to out-manoeuvre the enemy, who's trying to do exactly the same. Units are won and lost and eventually, perhaps several hours later, one person emerges the victor.

And already people's eyes are glazing over and their brains switching off, because it sounds so utterly mundane. Listen: it's really important that you give *Advance Wars* a chance to seduce you, because once you let it in your life it's very hard to get it out. Sure, it sounds like a measured, sedate experience, but you should never underestimate the euphoria in outsmarting someone, even a computer. And *Advance Wars: Dual Strike* teaches you to outsmart everyone in that coaxing way that Nintendo are oh so good at.

So how do you begin your military career? By learning how best to employ the forces of cute power that Nintendo put at your disposal, obviously. Everything has a strength and a weakness. Tanks are great at moving long distances, but can only attack next to an enemy. Rocket launches can strike from distance, but are weak and can't move many squares at once. Infantry is also easily destroyed, but can cross rivers and mountains which other units find unsurpassable.

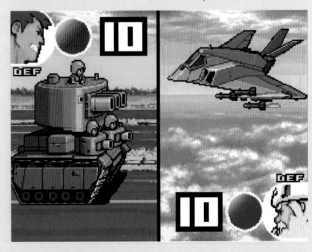

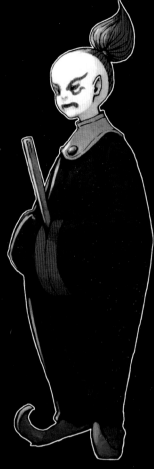

Learning the different types of terrain and how they affect the various parts of your army, too, is all part of the fun. But then there are so many other things that affect your game: the Commanding Officers, the weather, the particular ruleset used in the battle. So much to remember, so many options to consider, but since there's never a rush to make a move, always plenty of time to consider the wealth of things you can do.

And though, yes, it's still a military strategy game, it doesn't look like one. Other turn-based adventures litter their virtual boards with muddy pieces on brown terrain, but *Dual Strike*'s look is resolutely Nintendo. Tanks and planes are bright and cheerful, easily picked out from their surroundings and colour-coded with their allegiance. One glance at the screen can tell you the current state of play. It'll take substantially more glances than that for you to be absolutely sure you're making the right move.

That's the thing about this genre, and the *Advance Wars* series in particular: it has exactly the same sort of appeal as chess. That's unlikely to sell the game's glamorous side, admittedly, but like chess, it's about setting up a gameplay system which touches infinity. Particularly, the infinite variety afforded by the ways you can change your strategy which means that while you might be great, you can never be quite sure that you're the greatest. There's always another way you could have done things, and always the possibility that your victory might have been even quicker that way.

If infinite variety isn't compelling enough to make you consider involving yourself in war games, think about the amount *Advance Wars: Dual Strike* offers in terms of straight out single player action. Making your way through the main campaign takes long enough, but when you consider the extra maps you can buy to test your abilities, the extra commanding officers to unlock, and the host of game modes all of which can be tweaked to your combat preferences, it's a game that'll last forever.

All these superlatives can be applied to all of the games in the *Advance Wars* series (going back to its forefather,

Famicom Wars on the 8-bit NES). Each is brilliant, but what makes DS special is that you can use the touch-screen stylus, an interface that makes moving your troops around the *Advance Wars* universe even more instinctive than the traditional d-pad control. And, while the DS version introduces a host of complicated new options that some might find annoying, it's sensible enough to let you turn them all off if you want to. That preserves the simplicity of a game that's not just an elegant introduction to one of the most intimidating genres in gaming; it's the absolute pinnacle of it, too.

Play it now!

As it's a relatively new release it shouldn't be too tricky to find a copy of *Advance Wars: Dual Strike*, but if you've not bought a DS yet then there aren't too many fundamental differences between this version and the Game Boy Advance's *Advance Wars* and *Advance Wars 2*. Real retrogamers might want to try for the Japan-only *Famicom Wars*, released (unsurprisingly enough) for the Famicom.

Advance Wars™: *Dual Strike* © 2005 Nintendo/INTELLIGENT SYSTEMS

Animal Crossing™: Wild World

Publisher: Nintendo
Developer: Nintendo
Platform: Nintendo DS
Released: 2005

Moving into a new town isn't easy. You don't know anyone, there are new faces everywhere. The geography is completely unfamiliar. There are new customs to get used to, new places to visit and everyone's gossiping about people you've never heard of.

Also, they're all tiny, super sweet anthropomorphic animals, the taxi driver who brought you there is a somewhat crazy frog, and an over-enthusiastic raccoon seems to be trying to scam you out of some money.

Animal Crossing is Nintendo's wonderfully cute take on an open ended 'life' simulation. You start the game as your character moves into a village, and your aim is to live there. That's it, really. You just live life in a sweet cartoon town, and shape it so it's your fictional paradise.

Well, not just yours. There are around a dozen other inhabitants in your village, most with houses similar to your own, single-room creations with fun furniture and little cohesive style. The object, if there is an object in *AC*, is to be inspired by their home-owning pride, get a really nice house and furnish it to your will. You do that by earning money (bells) and buying nice furniture, and by paying off your mortgage and buying a bigger house. This is only the nominal aim. There is no actual aim in *Animal Cross-*

Nan

Have you seen my house? I spent a lot of time putting up those decorations...

Nintown
Nin

00,000

1/1 Mon
12 14 a.m.

ing: *Wild World*; you cannot complete it, and there is no end. There is just this overarching quest for a better place to live that you tell yourself you're trying to do, masking the bigger question. Why do you need a bigger house?

Well, so you can fit more furniture inside it, obviously. While that's true enough – bigger houses afford the opportunity to hoard much more junk, just like real life – the actual answer is that you don't *need* a bigger house. It's just an excuse to spend longer in *Animal Crossing*'s wonderfully benign universe. There is no real failure state here. Nothing really bad can happen to you. You might fall down a tiny hole and get a little red in the face trying to get out, or maybe you'll lose a few thousand bells on the stalk market and regret ever investing in turnips, but it's nothing you won't shake off in a few minutes of drinking in the sweet, sweet atmosphere.

Just like the original GameCube version, *Animal Crossing: Wild World* is tied into a hardware system clock, so when it's nighttime in the real world the sun goes down on your town in *Animal Crossing*, and when the shops open in the morning on your high street so Tom Nook, *Animal Crossing*'s in-game salesraccoon, opens his place for business too. More than that, it works off the DS's calendar. If you play the game on Halloween the

animals wear ghost costumes. If you play in autumn you'll find the leaves falling from the trees. If you play on your birthday you might be lucky enough to get presents. There are dozens and dozens of unique, day-specific events, and there's always a reason to play today and look forward to tomorrow. Equally, there's the fear that because you didn't switch the game on yesterday you missed something quietly amazing, something that won't come round again for a week, a month, a season, a year.

Specifically, your town in *Wild World* is full of insects and fish to catch. The types available to net and hook change with the time and the seasons, and you can donate them to the museum where curious, sleepy owl attendant Blathers will display them, offering brief, occasionally pithy commentary for every unique item. In order to provide Blathers with a complete collection you'll need to play the game all hours of the day and in every month, persistently chasing creatures around the pretty planet merely for the sake of catching them all. You will do that, too.

Just as you will patrol your village every day searching for fossils, which lie beneath the surface of the ground and turn into glorious dinosaur segments when presented to Blathers. You'll walk from animal to animal performing simple tasks which seem so mundane in isolation from the environment, but inside the world are perfectly natural, just like helping out a friend. You'll search Tom Nook's shop every single day for that vital piece of furniture you need to complete your perfect room theme; maybe you'll even put out a request on the internet for it, and use

Animal Crossing's excellent wi-fi facility to connect to someone else's village and trade with them.

You'll do all of these things to no particular end, just because Animal Crossing: Wild World is so well constructed, so finished, so impeccably, lovingly created that it's impossible not to love it too. It doesn't matter that there's nothing complicated to do (and there are many other simple diversions that haven't been mentioned here, like the letter writing aspects, and the constellations, and the clothes designing). You want to see everything there is to see because you know it'll have been coded with the same care and attention as the rest of the game, and it would be such a shame to miss it.

Perhaps the best way of summing up Animal Crossing is to give one last example of what you can do there. In the basement beneath the museum there's a coffee shop where a dog, KK Slider, comes to play tunes every Saturday evening. If you do not play Animal Crossing on Saturday evening you will not see his concert, you will never get to request anything, you will never receive a personal copy of his songs to play back at your place, and the coffee shop will always be empty to you. Well, mostly empty.

Because there's actually someone else there: a pigeon who's not really paying much attention to you, but stands behind the bar and serves coffee to anyone prepared to give him 200 bells. For that money – money you've worked hard for in the game – you get nothing more than the visual satisfaction of watching him make it and the big grin on your character's face after he's sipped it down. But you'll still do it. And you'll do it again and again, just because it really is so cute, so fun, so entertaining. That's Animal Crossing. No goal, no point, just pure love.

Play it now!

The easiest way to play Animal Crossing is to pick up a Nintendo DS and buy the game, which was released at the end of 2005 in the US and in spring 2006 in the UK. Those without a handheld system could try the GameCube version, which is still brilliant despite lacking some of the newer features (constellations, for example), but Europeans will have to import the US-only release from overseas.

Animal Crossing™: Wild World © 2005 Nintendo

Asteroids

Publisher: Atari
Developer: Atari
Platform: Arcade
Released: 1979

Whilst it's easy to declare the early generation of videogames as classics by default, few could argue that *Asteroids* has not aged well. Like many in its time, the hook was simple, the controls primitive and the visuals basic at best. But to this day, *Asteroids* stands proud against contemporary games – few of which will ever reach the levels of popularity as Atari's 1979, well, classic.

Released just a year after *Space Invaders*, *Asteroids* freed players from a ground-based spaceship, transporting them instead to the perils of infinite space. Players had to adapt quickly to a new style of play – one which rewrote the rules of spaceship combat.

If the rigid, relentless attack waves of *Space Invaders* proved predictable enough, *Asteroids* revelled in its randomness. The ship – inspired by the player's craft in the original videogame *Space War* – spawned in the centre of the screen, two large asteroids orbiting, slowly. When these asteroids were hit, they'd split into smaller versions, and then smaller still. Haphazard commanders could soon find their tranquil play area ruined by an over-enthusi-astic trigger finger – the skill was picking off these rocks systematically.

Control was handled with three buttons: rotate left and right, and thrust. Whilst an emergency 'hyperspace' button enabled players to displace themselves if they were in danger of being hit up the rear by an asteroid, cannier players used the screen wrap to manoeuvre out of trouble. In sticky situations, players simply zipped off the top or side of the screen to reappear at the opposite perimeter. Sadly, this temporal shift was available to the asteroids. And the UFOs.

Asteroids' reward was, as with all of the games at the time, in the high score table, and the associated bragging rights it offered. And these UFOs – which appeared at seemingly random points in the game – could offer huge bonuses to the sharpest shooters. As with *Space Invaders* before it, though, players soon worked out the algorithms dictating these extraterrestrial arrivals, using pre-discovered flaws in the code to generate them increasingly frequently. Early versions of the arcade cabinet even offered a safe spot behind the in-game score, though this was rectified in later revisions.

Whilst these early arcade games were credited with provoking a shortage of coinage in America and Japan, the videogames industry soon realised it had underestimated the demand. *Asteroids* was the first arcade cabinet to benefit from increased income storage – basically, the cabinets held more currency. The faster the banks manufactured coins, the quicker they were collated, pulling pennies from early morning to well into the night as the world gazed lovingly at the simple vector graphics.

To use a fairytale analogy, *Asteroids* boasted an ugly sister in the form of *Lunar Lander*, a game released for the

PUSH START

HIGH SCORES

1. 4880 BUM
2. 4650 POO

same base hardware in the same year. Whilst they shared certain similarities – the most obvious being the vector-based graphics and a 'thrust' button – their central premises were far apart. There was no 'fire' button in *Lunar Lander*, and in a Cold-War-paranoid world, the ability to blow up asteroid rock and the alien spacecraft would naturally find favour over a game which basically asked you to just park safely. As such, *Lunar Lander* cabinets were recalled and stripped of their innards in order to create more *Asteroids* machines. Now that never happened to Cinderella.

Such a global success was obviously going to spawn sequels. *Asteroids Deluxe* a year later offered a few visual tweaks and the introduction of a shield in favour of the random hyperspace function, and a fiercer alien foe which could fire more intelligently at the player. *Space Duel* came later the same year, but spoilt the original's simple appeal. The game's asteroids became colourful geometric shapes – hardly as menacing as the simple space rock. An early example of technology interfering for technology's sake.

Asteroids' legacy continued with *Pang!* – a game which can be best described as *Asteroids* crossed with *Space Invaders*. The enemies – balloons in this instance – split into smaller enemies, but the player was rooted firmly to the ground. A massive success in arcades and on home computers, *Pang!* proved that players like shooting big things into small things, and shooting them again some more. Like *Tetris* later, it's basically tidying up. Some joked that is why these games are so popular amongst girls – though the authors would certainly not share that perspective.

Many of the concepts introduced in *Asteroids* live on today. Tracing a gaming family tree with original designers Lyle Rains and Edd Logg as parents would produce an awful mess, at odds with their creation's beautiful simplicity. Among the offspring would be ancient games only the hardcore would recall – *Gravitar*, *Mad Planets* and *Sinistar*, to name but a few. Indeed, it could be argued that Xbox 360 launch title *Geometry Wars* is a modern reinterpretation of *Asteroids*, albeit one which uses the additional processing power to create a hugely popular title which hides its origins well.

But even with the bells and whistles of these modern versions, there's little doubt that the original game, with its minimalist visuals and simple controls, remains fiercely addictive. If you pass one by in a vintage arcade, beware its seductive charms and ensure you're not carrying coins you'll need later – as just one go is enough to be hooked. A walk home will soon seem more appealing than wasting money on bus fare.

Play it now!

Asteroids suffers the continued indignity of propping up compilations released on modern handheld formats. Atari Classics on DS boasts a faithful 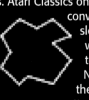 conversion, but the game's sloppy use of the Dual Screen won't impress those wishing to get the most from their Nintendo handheld, despite the fact that *Asteroids* plays pretty well. Like many of its turn-of-the-eighties arcade counterparts, *Asteroids* is also available on most modern phones. Older gamers may well want to forgo cost and convenience and treat themselves to an original cocktail cabinet on eBay.

Bangai-O

Publisher: Treasure/Swing!/Conspiracy Entertainment
Developer: Treasure Co.
Platform: N64, Dreamcast
Released: 1999

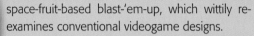

C hances are you won't have played *Bangai-O*. In fact, the chances are that you won't even have heard of it either. Its original Japanese release, on the Nintendo 64, was limited to a run of just 10,000 game cartridges, and although the Dreamcast version made it across to Europe and North America it was restricted to a similarly low print run. Since you probably haven't played it, you might be wondering how a game that looks like an unfashionably conventional 2D shoot-'em-up could possibly be considered one of the best games ever released. The answer is that it's not a conventional 2D shoot-'em-up. It's a gloriously ingenious, uniquely original, super destructive, exploding-with-energy reinvention of the space-fruit-based blast-'em-up, which wittily re-examines conventional videogame designs.

Or, as the back of the box puts it: 'Mind and skills level, unique shoot-'em-up with tasks found for the first time ever in a game like this.' An awesomely wayward translation that gives some hint of the barmy sense of surreality which ensues when you boot up the game. From start to finish, *Bangai-O* playfully defies expectations and tinkers with videogame cliché to create something startlingly original. The game's lead character, Riki, serves as a police officer with the 'people's police' next to his school. 'Naturally, these operations interfere with his grades at school,' deadpans the manual.

Character biographies are brilliantly nonsensical throughout. Take Montgomery, for example: 'A sheep from Mongolia which talks like pulp fiction. Appears to be harmless, but rambles on all day long.' Or Sabu, a weird looking blue guy: 'Unfortunately he is not very talented when it comes to preparing Takoyaki (octopus pellets) and

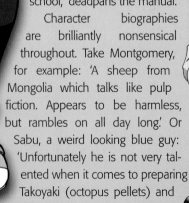

Hit me with your pointy stick

Rider while the continue screen depicts a naked Riki skipping after a candelabra-wielding hooded figure through a pastel-coloured garden. Dialogue sequences also feature hilarious non-sequiturs and frequently talk directly to the player. One tutorial message complains about the problem with 2D graphics; other conversations name-check the game's developer, Treasure; and the game's first boss exclaims: 'Are you at top speed or Just very small!' in a bizarrely punctuated observation about the game's unusually small sprites. Other bosses (including a trainee lawyer with a green sphere in place of a head) don't even fight back. Oh, and there are cheap puns, like a character called Nice Gai.

simply can not resist the waffles of the goldfish game salesman.' Or there's the super self-aware Black Riki (Riki's younger brother): 'After he found out that Riki is the main character of the game he challenged him since he always wanted to be the main character in a game.'

But *Bangai-O* isn't just nonsense for nonsense's sake: it also reaches outside itself, to reference all sorts of other games, cartoons and films, and it's full of visual absurdities. High score screens depict what appears to be Japanese TV icons Godzilla and Kamen

Unlike other shoot-'em-ups, smart bombs increase in effectiveness in proportion to the number of incoming enemy projectiles; they recharge in proportion to the amount of damage done by the player; and dealing lots of damage increases the likelihood of health recovery items appearing. The upshot of this is to place players on a gloriously counterintuitive knife edge: some of the game's most challenging levels require players to place themselves in the most hazardous circumstances in order to chain together gargantuan amounts of destruction to get to the end of the level.

In fact, level design is ingenious throughout, incorporating puzzles, mazes and all-out explosive fire fests, (and characteristically bonkers names like 'The space cemetery Exploding fruit store', and 'Only forwards from now on! like brand new cars'). One of the best levels requires the player to set off a series of fuses before racing against them to reach the end of the level before they burn out. Another leads the player to an apparent impasse, but careful exploration of the maze-like surroundings allows players to clear it.

Compared to this intense craziness, the game mechanics reveal themselves quite gradually. At the outset, the game appears to be quite conventional: shoot stuff, collect fruit to score points, and race to the boss encounter at the end of the level. Sure, the scale of destruction and action on screen is immensely satisfying, but that's all pretty standard stuff. Sure, it's nice to be able to swap between homing missiles and bouncing bullets, but that seems a pretty superficial feature at first. That is until successive levels require increasingly judicious selection of ammo, and the considered use of smart bombs – perhaps the game's single most satisfying hook.

Each new level provides another moment of realisation, revealing a little bit more about what makes *Bangai-O* so thrillingly novel and singularly extraordinary. Ironically though, this produces the game's only serious flaw: the fact that it has to come to an end. While each of the game's 44 levels provides plenty of replay value for high-score obsessives, there's nothing like the joyful novelty of encountering each level for the first time. So it's almost with a sense of sadness that the game's final (rock-hard) boss is eventually overcome. Which is actually the ultimate proof that the game is utterly, explosively amazing.

Bangai-O: N64/JP © TREASURE/ESP 1999. DC/JP © TREASURE/ESP 1999. DC/EU © 2000 TREASURE/ESP. Translation © 2000 Swing! DC/US © 2001 TREASURE/ESP. Translation © 2001 Conspiracy Entertainment

Play it now!

With *Bangai-O* limited to just 10,000 N64 cartridges and a similarly low number of Dreamcast discs, anybody wanting to sample the game today will need to stump up the exorbitant prices charged on eBay and other second-hand sources. It's definitely worth every penny, but given the popularity of games like *Mutant Storm* and *Geometry Wars* on Xbox Live Arcade here's hoping it will eventually be made available to the wider audience it deserves.

Battlefield 1942™

Publisher: Electonic Arts
Developer: Digital Illusions CE
Platform: PC
Released: 2002

From computerised pinball to global paintball, developer Digital Illusions' progression from small coding outfit formed by a bunch of Swedish demo programmers to one of the most lauded teams in the world has been entirely unpredictable. But when you're bought by Electronic Arts – the biggest publisher in the games business – you must be doing something right. And that something was Battlefield 1942, the title which can be credited with taking multiplayer gaming to an entirely new level. Literally.

Prior to its release in 2002, PC gamers who wanted to battle it out online were confined to ground-based combat. Vehicles were available in some titles, but it was Battlefield 1942 which introduced combat in a truly revolutionary way. For the first time, players were also able to fight in the skies and on water, commanding planes and ships alongside more standard infantry and ground-based vehicles. Heck, soldiers could control aircraft carriers, even.

Taking place in the Pacific and Atlantic theatres, Battlefield 1942 combined realistic visuals with a comic book approach to World War II. Players weren't restricted to classes – they could pretty much jump into the action at one of the pre-determined spawn points and immediately commandeer any available craft, or remain on foot if that more suited their style of play.

Whilst an offline mode catered for lone players without a modem by providing computer controlled 'bots' alongside which they could fight, it was the promise of online battles which really enthralled. Four different game modes each had different strategic and tactical emphases, but in all the overall goal was simple: do better than the opposing teams. The introduction of a team 'ticket' system struck a clever balance between infinite respawns and just a solitary life; every time a soldier died, the team's overall statistics were affected. As such, every member of the team had an overall responsibility to the group as a whole. A clever solution to what was then a thorny issue in the developing online gaming field.

Battlefield 1942's 16 maps drew inspiration from the conflict's most famous battles such as Omaha Beach, Stalingrad, Midway, Kursk and Berlin. Each location was optimised for playability rather than

Battlefield 2: Modern Combat *(Xbox 360, 2006) took the* Battlefield 1942 *concept and gave it a next-generation polish.*

Play it now!

Battlefield 2 on PC is perhaps the closest representation of the original game still being played, and is available widely at a reasonable price. Console owners will find *Battlefield Modern Combat* as polished as anything, if slightly more 'mainstream' in terms of presentation and mechanics. The third full release – *Battlefield 2142* – should be available on PC now.

Two 'total conversions' really shone through. *Galactic Conquest* swapped World War II conflict for battles set in the *Star Wars* universe. For the first time ever, it allowed players to take part in proper, squad-based first-person conflict using a range of troops, characters and vehicles from the *Star Wars* series. It was so professionally produced, it could be said this was the unofficial predecessor to commercial release *Star Wars Battlefront* (2004, multi-format).

The other total conversion which gained global recognition was *Desert Combat*, which took the series to the Middle East.

This mod proved so popular, the creators were acquired by Digital Illusions in 2004, and have worked in an official capacity on some elements of the game's sequel.

The sequel took the form of *Battlefield 2*, which was released in two separate guises for both PC and consoles in 2005 and 2006 respectively. Whilst the PC version – and subsequent expansion pack – have remained faithful to the original's vision, the console versions – subtitled *Modern Combat* – boast additional polish to cater for a console rather than computer demographic.

historical representation – which didn't win any awards for accuracy, but resulted in *Battlefield 1942* picking up a stack of accolades for gaming instead. Indeed, it pretty much swept the board of awards in 2003, collecting countless PC, online and overall game of the year gongs.

A couple of expansion packs went some way to keeping the game alive, and its community playing. *Road To Rome* (2003) added six tighter maps along with some additional vehicles. *Secret Weapons of WW II* (also 2003) introduced an even greater array of characters, weapons and options. Both enhanced the original game for a reasonable price, and by October 2003, it had sold over two million copies.

But these expansion packs were not the sole reason for keeping *Battlefield* servers busy. Digital Illusions released a software development kit (SDK) which enabled enthusiasts to alter practically every aspect of the game. A host of new downloads have subsequently appeared which transport the game to a variety of locations, from the high seas (*Battlefield: Pirates*), to the highways (*Battlefield: Interstate 1982*) and even into the world of toys (*Battlefield: GI Joe*).

With PCs and console becoming increasingly connected, many games now offer similar experiences to *Battlefield 1942*. But with *Battlefield 2*, Digital Illusions continues to illustrate that it understands the demands of computerised conflict like no other.

As the technology improves, squad-based combat will only get better and better, offering even greater levels, teams, weapons and vehicles. Many will continue to build on the genre invented by the *Battlefield 1942* developer. But only one can claim to have truly invented it.

Broken Sword: The Shadow of the Templars

Publisher:	Virgin Interactive/Sony Computer Entertainment Europe
Developer:	Revolution Software Ltd
Platform:	PC, PlayStation®
Released:	1996

The current global fascination with the legend of the Holy Grail – fuelled, of course, by Dan Brown's record-breaking *The Da Vinci Code* novel – shows little sign of abating. But years before the arrival of the book, movie and action figures, a similarly intriguing blend of historical conjecture and modern-day intrigue was appearing on millions of screens across the world – albeit computer monitors rather than silver ones.

Rather than asking its audience to passively consume its narrative, this tale was a perfect blend of interactive storytelling. And, as such, its place in our top 50 was guaranteed from the start.

Revolution Software's *Broken Sword: The Shadow of the Templars* introduced George Stobbard and Nico Collard, two characters whose will-they-won't-they? relationship has kept games players engaged for four games over a decade. Not bad for a tetchy American lawyer and irritable French journalist – two characters who individually would annoy, but together boast an astonishing chemistry.

The duo's arrival on-screen was marked with one of the adventure genre's most enduring memories. 'Paris in the Fall...' opens the story, as George recounts the tale which would take him from the French capital to locations in Ireland, Spain,

Syria and Scotland in a globe-spanning adventure which wove historical fact and fiction with a tight, modern plot and a substantial splash of humour.

From its explosive Parisian introduction to its dramatic conclusion in an ancient Scottish temple, *Broken Sword* is an adventure to savour. Right from the off, it was clear the game was leagues ahead of its peers, introducing cinematic-quality animations accompanied by a musical score by renowned composer Barrington Pheloung (*Inspector Morse*, *Hillary and Jackie*) within the opening seconds. The camera swoops across Paris's rooftops, down towards a café where George is enjoying a coffee. A clown appears, playing an accordion. It's a moment of tranquillity, of relaxation. Until the clown blows up the café in a dramatic, iconic gaming moment which remains as vivid today, a decade later.

Nothing remotely suspect about this guy

Broken Sword employed traditional hand-animation over wonderfully illustrated backdrops to portray a beautifully deadly world in which intrigue and danger were never far away. A perfectly paced narrative amused, entertained and thrilled in equal measures as players guided these two unlikely detectives and global saviours through a plot which would not look out of place at the top of the best seller list.

The game's simple interface – point and click refined – permitted surprisingly complex puzzles, rarely frustrating and always satisfying. A colourful cast of characters provided humour, intrigue and moments of high tension – unlike many of its contemporaries, players could die in *Broken Sword* if they made incorrect decisions at key moments. That players rarely became frustrated illustrates the strength of the game. Even those moments one would have to replay again were

rarely a chore. Apart from maybe the 'goat puzzle' – which proved so infuriating it remains infamous on internet forums and message boards to this day.

Unusually, *Broken Sword* appealed equally to both genders. *Broken Sword*'s success was, with hindsight, simple. It never dumbed down, even managing to ensure the historical conjecture remained entertaining. The exposition – portrayed, mainly, through cut-scenes between acts – rarely dragged, and the theories proposed about the bloodline of Christ encouraged additional reading. Anecdotal tales abound of *Broken Sword* players subsequently embarking on their own detective work at the game's denouement, becoming experts in the Knights Templar and the theory that Mary Magdalene married Jesus. Who knows – maybe a young Dan Brown completed the game?

At a time when home consoles were supposedly the choice of pill-popping clubbers, a PlayStation® version seemed a bold

The Goat Puzzle

One of the reasons the *Broken Sword* games have proved so popular is the consistency of the puzzles. If it wasn't evident, it was the player's ability to deduce the obvious clues at fault. Unlike so many American examples of the point and click genre, solutions were logical. Which is why the 'Goat Puzzle' proved the series' most frustrating moment.

In hindsight, it's clear – it's a timing puzzle. Watch the animation of the goat, and the order in which George should proceed is apparent. But this was the first time such a puzzle cropped up in the game, and, as such, it proved a stumbling block for many. The puzzle was simplified in the Game Boy Advance version, an admission it was too demanding for modern games players.

Broken Sword: The Sleeping Dragon *marked the series' first move into full 3D, bringing the world to life like never before.*

move. However, it was a refreshing entry in the young PlayStation® portfolio, proving a critical success despite the difficulties translating an interface initially designed for a mouse to a DualShock controller. Commercial success was hampered by a limited print run, as illustrated by the fact that second-hand copies were exchanging hands for more than they originally cost.

The series has proved a fertile ground for the Revolution team. In 1997, *Broken Sword 2: The Smoking Mirror* introduced the Mayan Prophecy to games players. The original was released on Game Boy Advance in 2002, whilst the third in the series – *Broken Sword: The Sleeping Dragon*, released in 2003 – added a third dimension and, somewhat controversially, dropped the point and click interface in favour of direct control.

Throughout it all, George and Nico have become embroiled in global conspiracies which, despite being entirely fictional, leave the player with lingering questions. Did Jesus really survive the crucifixion? What did happen to the Knights Templar? Will the world end in 2012 as the Mayans predicted?

But, most importantly: why haven't you two kissed?

Play it now!
Broken Sword: The Shadow of the Templars
(Astraware, Palm/Pocket PC, 2005)

Whilst the fourth game in the series may be grabbing the headlines, a fully preserved version of the game which started it all was published for Palm and Pocket PC PDAs in 2005. From the incidental animations to the wonderful score, everything which made the original so engrossing is now available in the palm of your hand. Indeed, some could argue this PDA release eclipses the original, with the point and click interface perfectly suited to a touchscreen. A fourth title in the series, *Broken Sword: The Angel Of Death*, is scheduled for release in late 2006, promising to reintroduce and modernise the stagnant point and click genre.

Call of Duty 2

Publisher: Activision
Developer: Infinity Ward, Inc.; PI Studios, LLC
Platform: PC, Xbox 360
Released: 2005

According to some online reports, a representative at *Call of Duty 2* publisher Activision is quoted as saying: 'We never set out to make the perfect World War II FPS to date.' Sadly for them – but happily for us – they failed. *Call of Duty 2* is, quite simply, the era's best first-person shooter on any format; an unrivalled single-player experience which recreates the horrors of WWII in terrifying yet highly entertaining fashion.

The game revels in set-piece after set-piece, pushing gaming boundaries further than ever before. After an introductory level in a basic training camp, players battle through a series of missions presenting the conflict from the perspective of the Russians, the British and, eventually, the Americans. Battles take place in Moscow, Stalingrad, El Alamein, Tunisia, Normandy, Libya, Bergstein and the Rhine. If it sounds like a

It's only a game, you'll keep reminding yourself. But some doubt will remain as you dodge artillery fire, see comrades fall in the most spectacular fashion, and dart over trenches in a bid to make the beach safe for incoming Allied craft.

Indeed, it's interaction with your comrades which really raises *Call of Duty 2* above the glut of WWII FPS titles. They'll fight alongside, reacting to your tactics, shouting advice and suggestions when not screaming for their lives. Whilst the endless regeneration of companion non-playing characters can shatter the illusion of realism, it's a necessary feature. Some games will punish players if NPCs bite the bullet. *Call of Duty 2* simply provides an infinite supply – of both companions and bullets.

Call of Duty 2 tweaked the traditional health pack system of its contemporaries, to some controversy. Whereas most games in the genre require players to pick up additional health when theirs is running low, *Call of Duty 2* introduced a system where if players ducked out of the firing line for a few seconds, they would completely recover. Even the absence of a health bar raised some eyebrows. But this

study session, that's intentional – each mission begins with an authoritative introduction courtesy of the History Channel.

If there's one thing players learn, it's that the war must have been hell. But in high-definition and Dolby surround sound, it's also pretty beautiful.

There's little time to admire the view, though. Whether it's the snowy wastes of Russia or the imposing cliffs of Normandy, levels are populated with flying bodies, bullets and shells. Rubble shatters, the ground disappears – it's a game which requires patience as well as derring-do. Seek cover when available; when it's not, keep moving.

The Normandy Landing level in particular illustrates the game's design and power in one hellish mission. Of course, this sequence has been recreated before in many a game – but never with the incidental touches of *Call of Duty 2*.

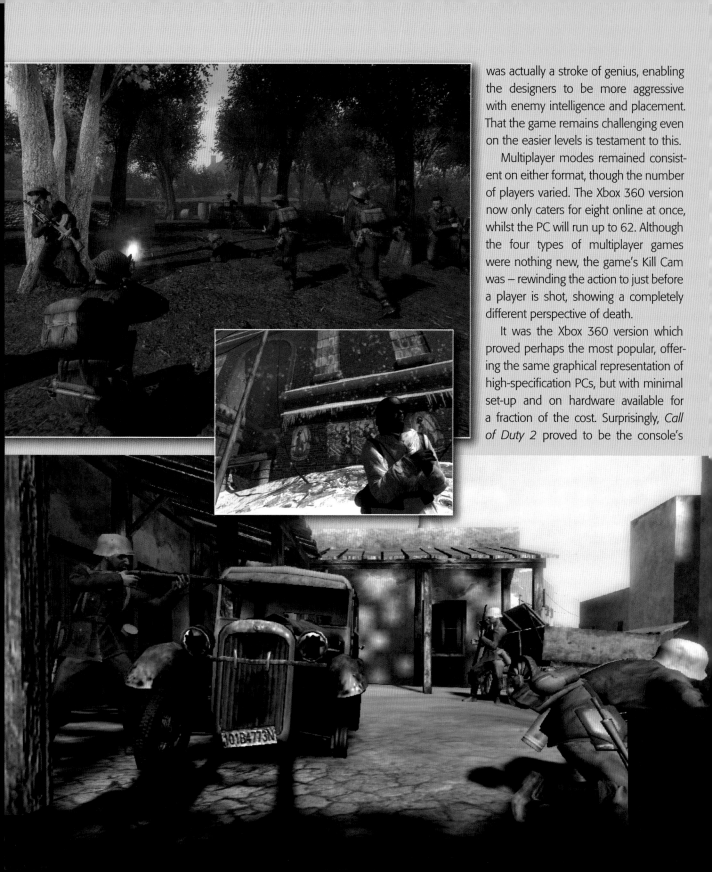

was actually a stroke of genius, enabling the designers to be more aggressive with enemy intelligence and placement. That the game remains challenging even on the easier levels is testament to this.

Multiplayer modes remained consistent on either format, though the number of players varied. The Xbox 360 version now only caters for eight online at once, whilst the PC will run up to 62. Although the four types of multiplayer games were nothing new, the game's Kill Cam was – rewinding the action to just before a player is shot, showing a completely different perspective of death.

It was the Xbox 360 version which proved perhaps the most popular, offering the same graphical representation of high-specification PCs, but with minimal set-up and on hardware available for a fraction of the cost. Surprisingly, *Call of Duty 2* proved to be the console's

biggest hit during the first few weeks the Xbox 360 was on sale, beating Microsoft's format-exclusive first-person shooter *Perfect Dark Zero* across the globe. The game generated revenues of over 15million dollars in its first week on sale in the States – a staggering figure, made even more impressive when you consider it was bought by four out of every five Xbox 360 owners during the launch week.

In just two short years, *Call of Duty 2* greatly improved over almost every element of its predecessor. With a sequel in the works, one cannot imagine how things will advance between now and its release. *Call of Duty 2* recreates WWII's most famous battles in harrowing, hideous, nightmarish glory. Bodies fly, comrades fall. Vision blurs and eardrums burst. There are times when it becomes totally overwhelming. But you'll always find yourself going back for more.

Play it now!

One of the most modern games in the top fifty, *Call Of Duty 2* remains widely available on both PC and Xbox 360. By the time of publication, it should be available at a discount, so if you don't own it already, there's no excuse.

Call of Duty 2 © 2005 Activision Publishing, Inc.

Command & Conquer™

Publisher: Virgin Interactive
Developer: Westwood Studios
Platform: PC
Released: 1995

Wouldn't it be nice to get on with the neighbours … Red Alert.

Command & Conquer remains one of the most significant PC releases of the nineties, simultaneously establishing the real-time strategy genre and stabilising the home computer as a viable gaming platform when it was under attack from a new generation of consoles. Most importantly, it created a whole new generation of games players who demanded – and continue to demand – something more cerebral in their interactive entertainment. Not bad for a non-licensed title from a developer which was up until then primarily renowned for a Dungeons & Dragons role-playing game.

Published in 1995, Command & Conquer was essentially a superficial enhancement of Westwood Studios' previous title Dune 2, hiding its similarities beneath the shiny new technologies that were becoming increasingly commonplace in PCs. Increased graphical capabilities, enhanced sound and

a (then) whopping 600-odd megabytes of CD-ROM storage enabled developer Westwood Studios to produce a game which played and felt exactly how they must have imagined during predecessor Dune 2's initial brainstorming session.

Westwood took Dune 2's premise and transposed it from sci-fi desert wasteland to a more popular setting. Command & Conquer took place in the near future, in a world torn apart by global conflict. Players picked a side and battled through the game from the perspective of the beige-coloured Global Defense Initiative (GDI) or the red Brotherhood of NOD – two opposing factions who used widely differing tactics to strive for victory.

The good GDIs comprised an alliance of the world's most powerful nations, the bad Brotherhood, a renegade band of

It was the control system – dubbed the 'Command & Conquer' interface during the development of *Dune 2* – which proved so revolutionary. Refined from *Dune 2*, its potentially baffling array of options was cleverly structured to offer players choices appropriate to each moment in the game.

Each level played in a similar fashion. Players began each battle with a limited knowledge of their surroundings, the majority of the level shrouded in a 'fog of war'. Exploration uncovered the detail within the map – but took time and resource. Multi-tasking was required from the off as players juggled the construction of a secure base with sufficient protection with the demands of assembling an army to go on the offensive and wipe out the opposition.

Whilst *Command & Conquer* offered the player seemingly unlimited strategies, progression was dictated by the order in which players constructed individual factories. For example, building a barracks opened up additional opportunities, allowing players to initially order relatively weak minigun and grenade infantry, eventually progressing to hard-as-nails commandos who could single-handedly storm enemy buildings.

terrorists headed by the self-appointed leader Kane. Whilst the thrust of the game was a series of head-to-head battles across the planet, the objective was the same no matter what the team's colours: to harvest and control significant amounts of Tiberian – a valuable substance with mysterious genetic-altering properties.

COMMAND & CONQUER

Harkonnen Troopers.

TROOPERS

DMG

ATTACK
MOVE
RETREAT
GUARD

Select your next conquest

Select your next region

Do you wish to join House Atreides?

Yes   No

**Dune 2 *(1992, PC)*: the blueprint for Command &
Conquer. *Despite there being just three years between
them, the advances in technology are visually obvious.***

A helipad opened up aerial opportunities, whilst other buildings allowed scientific research, producing increasingly powerful and advanced weaponry and defences. Above all this, the need to balance construction and research expenditure against the value of the harvested Tiberian which governed the game's economy. Indeed, often it was financial mismanagement which could prevent a commander conquering all.

This wonderful choreography of war would not have been possible had the interface failed. Whilst keyboard shortcuts were available, players could progress through the game using two mouse buttons and a left or right click. The screen free from clutter, the majesty of global conflict was presented like never before, freeing players to concentrate on strategies rather than cumbersome menus, egged on throughout the game by the wonderfully seductive in-game commentator. 'Your base is under attack' has never sounded so lovely.

Of course, this progressive gameplay had been seen before, but until *Dune 2* it was turn-based. So whilst realtime strategy games arrived with its predecessor, it was *Command & Conquer* which provided a global bang.

A huge success, the *C&C* series subsequently spawned spin-off titles. *Command & Conquer Red Alert* (1996) took the war back to an alternative history, where Einstein invents a time-machine to prevent Hitler from winning World War II. Rather than fixing things, however, Einstein's machinations produce a new threat: a world in which the Soviets have risen unchecked. *Command & Conquer: Sole Survivor* was a more ambitious attempt at moving the series to a new level. Ahead of its time, it was multiplayer-only and generally poorly received. Finally, *Command & Conquer: Renegade* (2003) presented the familiar structure from an unfamiliar viewpoint, moving to third-person for a more immediate view of the conflict.

As is often the case, as the series progressed, the original team members began to fragment, buoyed by their critical and financial successes. Some formed new studios, others simply walked away. Innovation in the genre has typically come from new teams and new franchises. That said, a third *Command & Conquer* is well into development and scheduled for release in 2007. The developers are promising to take the popular series back to its roots in the Tiberium universe with a gripping story that will 'redefine storytelling in RTS games.'

The outcome remains to be seen. But whatever the result, in the overall scheme of gaming, what *Dune 2* started and *Command & Conquer* advanced cannot be understated. The real-time strategy mechanic is now applied to all sorts of licences, all sorts of scenarios. Whether it's by name or not, there's little doubt that every RTS still retains a little bit of *Command & Conquer*.

He shoots... he scores! Goaaaal!

Play it now!

Command & Conquer: The First Decade (PC, Electronic Arts, 2006)
Electronic Arts – which bought developer Westwood Studios in 1998 – released *Command & Conquer: The First Decade* in early 2006. This mammoth package contains almost every title ever released in the series. Whilst some players have experienced teething problems on modern PCs, the individual games still prove hugely enjoyable, with the overall pack providing the most definitive anthology of the series to date. *Command & Conquer: Sole Survivor* is, perhaps wisely, omitted from the pack.

Dance Dance Revolution

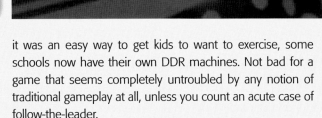

Publisher: Konami
Developer: Konami
Platform: Arcade, PS2, Xbox, GameCube
Released: 1998

Arcade games are few and far between in this book, partially thanks to the arcade industry's painful decline over the last decade. But if there's one game that defines the modern face of coin-operated gaming it's *Dance Dance Revolution*, the huge metal structure that's an unmistakable feature of every remaining arcade across the world. Not only that, but it is the quintessential rhythm action game, the franchise that defined a genre and sold a million dancemats. It even gave gaming a positive spin; noticing that

it was an easy way to get kids to want to exercise, some schools now have their own DDR machines. Not bad for a game that seems completely untroubled by any notion of traditional gameplay at all, unless you count an acute case of follow-the-leader.

One of the tenets of good game design is that the player should have as much opportunity to interact with his or her surroundings as possible. In *Dance Dance Revolution* you do not tell the game what to do at any point. It tells you what to do, you listen, and you obey. It doesn't sound like the most attractive idea on paper, but then it's not a pen and paper game. It's one of the most physical experiences gaming has to offer.

Here is how it works. The player stands in the middle of a dancemat with four arrows surrounding them: up, down, left and right. A sequence of garishly glowing arrows begins at the bottom of the screen and moves up towards a row of translucent arrows at the top. As the bright arrows hit the translucent arrows one by one, so the player must step on the appropriate arrow on the floor beneath them. If they perform the step at exactly the right moment the game screams encouragement over the top of the music. If they fail, the game has no qualms about telling them so, and we move quickly on to the next arrow, perhaps only a bar away, or a beat or a quarter of a beat or already there, depending what difficulty is being played.

It's a non-stop disco party, apparently

So that is your dancing revolution: game tells the player where to move their feet, and so the player starts to dance. It's a strange type of dancing, maybe somewhere between morris dancing and breakdancing, informing sharp, aggressive movements of the legs and a peculiar type of flow. As players get better the form they take becomes looser, faster and more rhythmic, and so they become increasingly creative. They learn that the *Dance Dance Revolution* pad cannot distinguish between a hit from a foot and a hit from any other part of the body, and much of the thrill in the game at later stages comes from using your elbows, knees and even your head to touch the floor pad.

(It's interesting to note that when players get incredibly good at *Dance Dance Revolution*, so good that even the highest levels provide little challenge for them, it's not uncommon for them to turn the difficulty level down to something more reasonable and try and do that routine while performing the most spectacular dancing possible. Not that watching an expert perform the highest levels isn't spectacular in and of itself, but it's more like watching *Riverdance* on fast forward, impressive but not obviously cool.)

It's entirely possible you could become one of those players, even with no dancing talent whatsoever. After playing *DDR* for a while you'll start to notice that your legs are moving on their own. It's perhaps the best example there is of the way gaming informs muscle memory, that peculiar state where you no longer have to think about what you're seeing on screen, where you just let the arrows float from in front of you to your feet. You start to see the arrows not as individual directions but as musical phrases, clumps of grouped directions that tell your whole body how to shift, spin and dance.

The way the game expresses the moves is something that's been tinkered with by dozens of imitators, too, but none are as effective in moving your feet as Konami's original. The only question left is where to start, and there's no clear answer to that. There are dozens of versions of *Dance Dance Revolution*, and no definitive

version as the base mechanic is largely identical. Which you prefer comes down as much to the music you like dancing to as much as anything. Those who enjoy jumping to sickly-sweet Japanese techno will have the widest choice, but in truth, it doesn't matter too much even if the music isn't for you. The beat is the important part; that, and making yourself look vaguely ridiculous in the name of gaming compulsion. And hey, who wouldn't find that idea attractive?

Play it now!

There is no shortage of ways to play *Dance Dance Revolution*, with versions existing for every major gaming format. You'll need a mat first, and it's worth being wary of the cheaper brands, whose response times vary wildly and can make the game frustrating to the degree of pointlessness.

Dance Dance Revolution © Konami Corporation. All Rights Reserved.

Dead or Alive 4

Publisher: Microsoft
Developer: Tecmo
Platform: Xbox 360
Released: 2005

D ead or Alive 4 was the first best advert for Microsoft's Xbox 360, and one of the first best adverts for its newly enhanced Xbox Live service. Held back from launch so that Tomonobu Itagaki's Team Ninja could deliver a scintillatingly beautiful, supremely balanced beat-'em-up, it swiftly established itself as the poster boy (or, more appropriately, girl) of online multiplayer competition. And it brought the beat-'em-up kicking and countering into the brave new world of high definition visuals with jaw-dropping (and jaw-smashing) aplomb. Oh, and it happens to feature some of the hottest girls ever seen in a videogame.

Ahh, the girls. Female players might feel aggrieved at the rather limited selection of beefcake on offer (unless they've got a thing for the dubious biker-chic of Bass, or the mature mystique of Gung Fu). But the majority of males will probably head straight to the settings page and ramp up their age to 99 to enjoy a not-so-secret feature which heightens the amount of (ahem) 'bounce' on display. Certainly the girls look undeniably great – and while the end-game boss is fiendishly and almost unfairly difficult to beat, at least she's got a nice ass. But dedicated pervs would probably be better off sticking to *Dead or Alive Xtreme Beach Volleyball*. *DoA 4* is all about combat.

When it launched, *DoA 4* entered an arena dominated by big name brawlers like *Tekken*, *Soul Calibur*, *Mortal Kombat* and *Virtua Fighter*. Nevertheless, it dis- tinguished itself by doing everything that all the best beat-'em-ups do, but by doing it all superbly well. Kick, punch, block and throw add up to super fast combos and high tempo bouts; a rich and colourful roster of characters employ a wide range of contrasting fighting styles; and there are more play modes and unlockable characters and costumes than you can shake a stick at.

The quality of Dead or Alive's visuals hadn't been seen on a home console before the Xbox 360

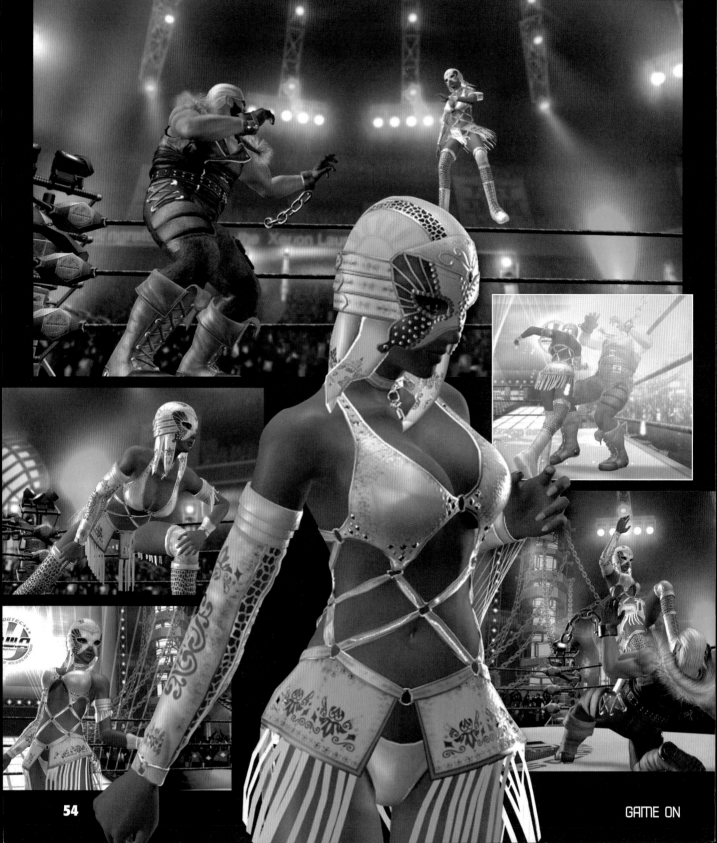

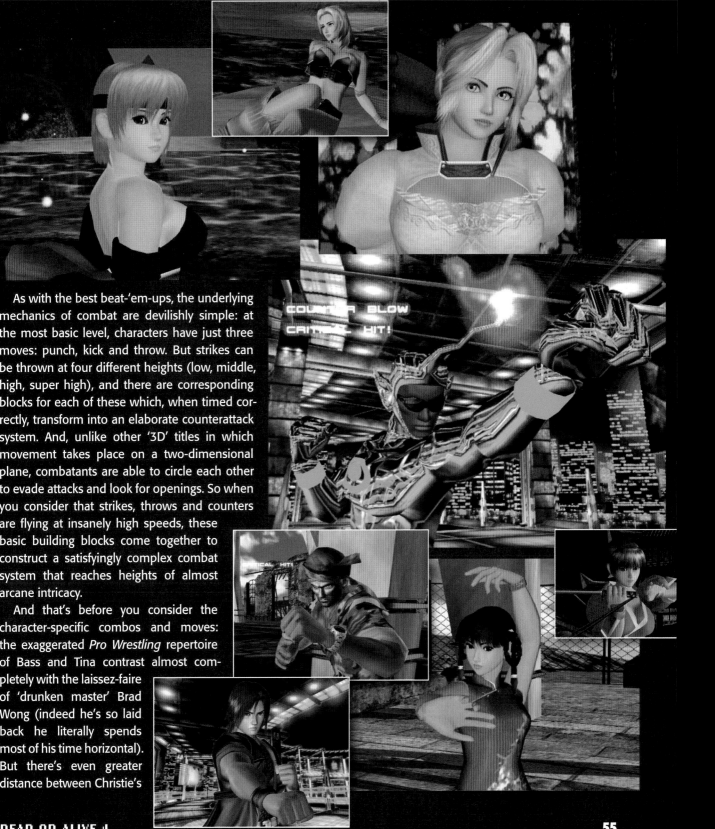

As with the best beat-'em-ups, the underlying mechanics of combat are devilishly simple: at the most basic level, characters have just three moves: punch, kick and throw. But strikes can be thrown at four different heights (low, middle, high, super high), and there are corresponding blocks for each of these which, when timed correctly, transform into an elaborate counterattack system. And, unlike other '3D' titles in which movement takes place on a two-dimensional plane, combatants are able to circle each other to evade attacks and look for openings. So when you consider that strikes, throws and counters are flying at insanely high speeds, these basic building blocks come together to construct a satisfyingly complex combat system that reaches heights of almost arcane intricacy.

And that's before you consider the character-specific combos and moves: the exaggerated Pro Wrestling repertoire of Bass and Tina contrast almost completely with the laissez-faire of 'drunken master' Brad Wong (indeed he's so laid back he literally spends most of his time horizontal). But there's even greater distance between Christie's

obscure Kung Fu style She Quan and unlockable *Halo* character Spartan-458's sci-fi plasma grenades and power armour. Yet the beauty of *Dead or Alive 4* is that it manages to incorporate and differentiate these disparate styles without upsetting the competitive balance of the game (along with Karata, Sambo, Tai Chi, Lucha Libre and Ninjutsu among others).

So *DoA* does everything really well, and looks great. What it does really differently, though, is to do it all online, and in multi-tiered, interactive arenas. Other games might feature pretty environments, but none of them really add such a layer of tactical depth: combatants crash each other into stone walls or electrified barriers; throw their opponents down stone

temple stairs or through paper walls; fruit stands smash and scatter their contents underfoot; and passing cars and (rather oddly) dinosaurs provide the occasional hazard.

More significant, though, is the game's online aspect. While it was possible to play previous versions of *Dead or Alive* over the original Xbox Live, *DoA 4* epitomises the 360's new Xbox Live service to take it to a new level. Players can customise their own avatar by visiting Zack's Shop, and receive rankings according to their level of success. More notable is the implementation of Microsoft's new Game Achievements system to encourage players to attempt to put together mammoth winning streaks, or interrupting those of others: some achievements reward virtuoso performances; some achievements mock those who are below par.

It's rumoured that Tomonobu Itagaki enlisted the help of professional *DoA* players during the game's development to ensure the perfect balance. Perhaps one drawback of this approach is that the game is punishingly difficult, and it makes no concessions to newcomers (or even players familiar with previous titles). But you'll find yourself unable to stop yourself from picking your controller up off the floor and starting again: master the moves and the high-speed tempo, and *Dead or Alive* is enormously rewarding.

Play it now!
You can play *Dead or Alive 4* and its Xbox predecessor, *Dead or Alive 3* today on Xbox 360.

Dead or Alive 4 images reprinted with permission from Microsoft Corporation.

The Elder Scrolls® IV: Oblivion™

Publisher: T2K Games
Developer: Bethesda Software
Platform: Xbox, PC
Released: 2006

One thousand years ago, when men were men and dragons were dragons and those men killed those dragons because that was what men were born to do, when electricity was chiselled from lumps of coal thrown on the fire and computers were the size of oxen and powered by hand cranks, here is how the social order was written: people who played videogames were shaggy beasts who loved nothing more than adventuring in fake medieval worlds and living Tolkien-style adventures to the full. Things have changed, of course, and gaming's a touch more socially acceptable these days. But those sort of games live on, and the *Elder Scrolls* series has been carrying the baton for many a year. *Oblivion* is their pinnacle.

Or their lowest ebb, depending on where you stand on the joy of elves and orcs. This is a traditional role-playing game with few concessions to openness or accessibility; you can tell that right from the start, because creating your character, delicately shaping their experience and allocating strength and skills across various categories, is an intricate and time-consuming business. It's an obsessive compulsive nightmare, allowing you to configure every single aspect of their being, from their skill as

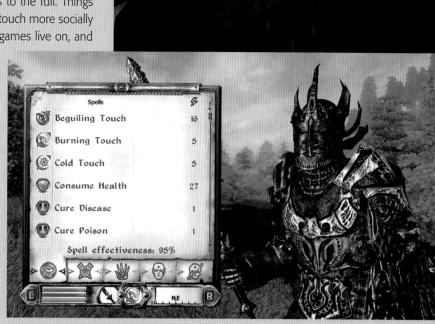

THE ELDER SCROLLS IV: OBLIVION

a blacksmith to the prominence of the bridge of their nose. But once you've created your hero (and led him or her through an hour-long tutorial dungeon crawl) the game opens up into a huge, epic adventure whose scale is almost unprecedented.

This is a huge landscape, hundreds of dungeons squirrelled away beneath obscure hills for you to seek out and conquer. And when you're bored of the main mission, which takes you o'er hill and vale and through hellish Oblivion gates into otherworldly realms, you can amuse yourself by just living the sort of life dreamt of at Renaissance fairs the world over. Become a thief and break into houses, or embark on helpful side-quests for profit and pleasure. Find yourself playing the part of a private investigator, conducting your own country-wide investigations into murder and misdeed. Kill everyone that moves, or try and work your way into the upper ranks of the mages guild. Or do all of those things and never find the time to get anywhere near completing the game. The beauty

of *Oblivion* is that it really doesn't care. The world is your plaything.

So how do you play? Any way you want would be the simple answer, but the common theme to all play styles is this: exploration. Whether it's exploration brought on by the game's main quests sending you from location to location, or exploration formed from your own inquisitive nature, much of *Oblivion*'s thrill comes from virtual tourism. And like real-world tourism, the greatest thrill is in finding something amazing for yourself. The world is so, so huge, and it's almost insulting to imagine just keeping to the beaten paths that criss-cross the landscape. Skipping from them for even a minute produces magical gaming moments, moments where it feels like you're genuinely a pioneer. Find a treasure chest squirrelled beneath a tree stump and pick the lock. Drink in the genuine sense of anticipation as it creaks open.

Exploration isn't without its perils, of course. On your way around the *Elder Scrolls'* luscious landscape you'll

Play it now!

A high spec PC will allow you to play *Oblivion*, and to take advantage of the hundreds of free modifications on offer, put together by the RPG community. Alternatively, the Xbox 360 version has bite-sized add-ons that can be purchased through Xbox Live, expanding the game's life at pocket-money cost.

encounter all manner of enemies, from the meagre mud-crabs through to hellish beasts from the nightmarish land of Oblivion. That's the hook in the game: fire-spitting portals are appearing throughout the land and it's your job to go through them and fight off the oncoming hordes. Though you occasionally receive support in the form of (slighty stupid, mostly gung-ho) NPCs, the majority of the time you adventure alone, and you kill alone too.

Combat is broadly a test of timing, but again depends on how you choose to play the game. If you're an archer, you can expect to spend most of your time sniping from a distance, trying to inflict as much damage on an enemy before they get close enough to involve you in melee combat. The same thing goes if you're a heavy magic user, unless you prefer to specialise in the touch spells which affect your opponent's constitution on contact. Warriors will eschew any subtlety for out-and-out violence, getting up close and personal with their broadswords, while thieves may sneak through darkened corridors to inflict critical blows on unsuspecting enemies. Some players may choose to mix and match, each skill improving with use and turning their character into a jack of all trades, but perhaps a master of none. Whatever, the experience of even the simplest, combat-only dungeon crawl is wildly different depending on how you play the game.

Most of the quests are much more than that, and the freedom is intoxicating. Beyond the ability to do anything there is nothing here that defies gaming convention, only reinforces it. Is that bad? No. *Oblivion* knows it's a geek and really doesn't care because it's so very good at it. It is the absolute pinnacle of every bad thing you've ever been told about videogames: an insular, arcane, unashamedly nerdy experience for the resolutely anti-social. And it's absolutely brilliant.

elite

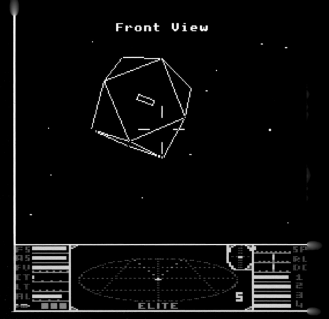

Front View

Publisher: Acornsoft/various
Developer: Ian Bell and David Braben
Platform: BBC, various others
Released: 1984

The world was a very different place in 1984. Mobile phones were literally the size of bricks. The internet was still a military research project and the World Wide Web just a distant dream. Ronald Reagan and Margaret Thatcher enjoyed a 'special relationship', and maintained a united front against the Soviet Union. *Ghostbusters* and *The Terminator* played in movie theatres, and *Miami Vice* on telly. More importantly, computer games came on audio cassettes which had to be loaded into memory every time they were played. *Your Computer* magazine was predicting the demise of newfangled input device 'the mouse'. And yet, in the space of just the 32k of memory available on the BBC Micro, two Cambridge students created a game that spanned eight galaxies and over 2,000 planets. Its name was *Elite*, and it would change the face of videogames forever.

Although its wireframe visuals were cutting-edge, it wasn't the first game to feature 3D graphics – arcade game *I Robot* had earlier featured vectors and polygons. Similarly, although it was the first action game that allowed players to save their progress and resume over successive sessions of play, early text adventures had included a similar feature. But in creating a truly open-ended space opera, incorporating pan-galactic trading, space combat in three dimensions, countless ship upgrades, and more than one passing reference to the sci-fi satire of Douglas Adams, *Elite* bucked the commercially dominant trend of quick-fix 2D arcade games like *Defender* and *Pac-Man*. It also inspired a whole genre of space shooters characterised by series such as *Wing Commander* and *TIE*

```
COMMANDER JAMESON

Present System        :Lave
Hyperspace System     :Lave
Condition             :Docked
Fuel:7.0 Light Years
Cash:      100.0 Cr
Legal Status: Clean
Rating: Harmless

EQUIPMENT:
        Front Pulse Laser
```

Fighter and *X-Wing*, which dominated the scene during the early nineties. More significantly, it created a template for the sandbox worlds of some of today's biggest blockbusters, such as *Grand Theft Auto* and *Elder Scrolls IV: Oblivion*.

The game took its title from a series of ranks that players earned in combat. Starting outside Lave Space Station with just 100 Credits and a lightly armed trading ship, the Cobra Mark III, players could increase their combat rating from Harmless to Elite (via other ranks like Mostly Harmless and Dangerous) by achieving a certain number of kills. If the game could be said to have any sort of defined goal, this was probably it. But there was much more to the game than just combat. The game's open-ended universe featured military missions, bounty hunting, mining, shooting, exploration, trade and even piracy (surely an appropriate theme given the number of schoolchildren who experienced the game via a cracked copy and a hastily scrawled list of likely passwords).

In many ways, though, the story behind the creation of the game is almost as interesting as the action that unfolds each time you play the game. Its unlikely creators Ian Bell and David Braben met in October 1982 at Jesus

College Cambridge, where they were studying Maths and Physics respectively, and they had only started programming, in BASIC, just a few years earlier. Gravitating to the more complicated assembly language, they created the game over the course of 18 months, working in tandem, dividing programming tasks between them at a time when it was more usual for games to be created by only one individual.

The pair started out with the idea of creating a 3D space combat game, but added the notion of trade to fill out the universe. It proved to be an inspired decision, but still didn't impress the first publisher that the pair pitched to. According to Braben, Thorn EMI's rejection letter said: 'the game needs three lives, it needs to play through in no more than about 10 minutes, users will not be prepared to play for night after night to get anywhere, people won't understand the trading, they don't understand 3D, the technology's all very impressive but it's not very colourful.'

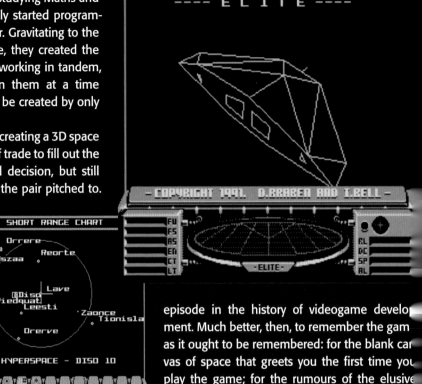

Not a decision that would be vindicated by hindsight: the game's eventual success spanned 17 different formats, and sales of around a million – indeed sales of the original BBC Micro version reached a total of almost 150,000 virtually one copy for every BBC Micro in existence!

No doubt part of that success is attributable to publisher Acornsoft's decision to package the game in a bigger box than usual, so that they could include a host of goodies: in the box were the game and its manual, but also a chart, some stickers, and a postcard for players to register their Elite status with. There was even a novella, *The Dark Wheel*, written by Robert Holdstock.

There was a dark side, though, to the overnight success which propelled the two young men into the realms of the rich and famous. Two sequels created by David Braben's Frontier Developments without the involvement of Ian Bell generated an ugly spat between the two, involving disputes about royalties and attempts to sue for libel. It was an unfortunate end to an otherwise illustrious

episode in the history of videogame development. Much better, then, to remember the game as it ought to be remembered: for the blank canvas of space that greets you the first time you play the game; for the rumours of the elusive Generation Ship; for the first time you attempted to dock with a spinning space station; for a game that was truly pregnant with possibilities; and as a momentous occasion in the history of computer games.

Play it now!

David Braben has mooted the possibility of creating another chapter in the *Elite* universe, but has kept fans waiting for more information since 1998. With no sign of its imminent arrival, anyone who wants to sample the original *Elite* or its sequels for themselves can do so by downloading one of the many emulated or shareware versions that are freely available on the internet – from Ian Bell's website (www.iancgbell.clara.net/elite/pc/index.htm) for example, or Elite Club (www.eliteclub.co.uk/). And should you want to read *The Dark Wheel* to complete the experience, it's currently available to read on Ian Bell's website: www.iancgbell.clara.net/elite/dkwheel.htm

EyeToy® Play

Publisher: Sony Computer Entertainment Europe
Developer: London Studios
Platform: PlayStation® 2
Released: 2003

Whilst most gamers feel absolutely comfortable with a PlayStation® DualShock controller between their hands, those picking one up for the first time can be forgiven for feeling a little overwhelmed. Whereas the early home consoles boasted one or two buttons and a single joystick shaft, modern games tend to use every available button or stick, which can prove too much for someone new to the medium. Indeed, many have argued that games are asking too much from their players; that the complexities of next generation controllers present a barrier to entry for first-time players.

One radical solution is to do away with the controller altogether. A bold move, for sure – but one tested by Sony Computer Entertainment to tremendous success with its *EyeToy* series of games, the first of which – *EyeToy: Play* – was released in 2003.

The game was the brainchild of Richard Marks, now special projects manager at Sony US. When working as a start-up developer in 1999, he'd seen the unveiling of the PlayStation® 2 at a game development conference – his naturally curious mind began imaging the new ways this technology could potentially be used. He submitted a paper to Sony's R&D department, and the result is a game which, in Europe, sold over one million copies in four months.

EyeToy: Play comprises 12 simple games and one small camera which sits on top of the user's television. Provided there's sufficient light and a suitable static background, the technology can determine which areas of its vision are moving. So instead of moving left or right with a joystick, players wave a hand, leg or any other available part of the body. The visuals from the camera are integrated with the PlayStation®-generated imagery, putting players actually in the game themselves. The result is a title which can be enjoyed by all.

EyeToy focused on simple activities. *Keep Ups* presented a bouncing football, challenging players to keep the ball in the air by juggling it off their knee, leg, head and even arms – though that, obviously, is not in the spirit of football. *Boxing Champ* allowed players to punch a virtual opponent. And *Wishi Washi* simply asked players to clear a screen of suds within a set time limit. Who'd have thought virtual window cleaning would prove so popular?

If it sounds ridiculous on paper, it's even more so in practice. Tales abound of enthusiastic PlayStation® owners forgetting exactly what they're doing and standing in front of windows, causing curious neighbours to wonder what all that strange gyrating is all about. Yet that's the point: *EyeToy: Play* is very much a party game, designed to be enjoyed in a social setting with friends or family. If you're not actually playing yourself, it's often as much fun to watch someone else doing so. High scores – complete with pictures saved for posterity – provide the long-term challenge.

Games development and publishing is a risk at the best of times. Millions of dollars are invested up front, and predicting sales is a tricky business. *EyeToy: Play* in particular was a massive financial gamble for Sony. It needed to order – and pay for – the USB cameras in advance, in what was a considerable outlay. Whilst its failure would not have proved fatal for the publisher, some serious questions would be raised at board and shareholder level.

But some ideas – no matter how ludicrous – are worth believing in, and Sony's faith was justified as legions of new games players were tempted by *EyeToy*'s premise. The game sold tremendously well over an extended period of time, bucking the trend of the majority of titles whose sales typically decline after the opening weekend. Two sequels were released offering further energetic delights, and additional games in the *EyeToy* series such as *AntiGrav* and *Kinetic* have presented additional themed minigames compatible with the camera.

Most impressively, *EyeToy* is now a format in its own right. Even rival developers and publishers have been incorporating the technology into separate games, presenting bonus content for those with the necessary equipment.

A similar peripheral has been announced for Xbox 360. And whilst there's no camera included as standard, Nintendo's Wii console offers gesture control surely inspired by *EyeToy*. What could have become a gaming oddity has actually changed the way people interact with interactive entertainment, opening up the delights of console gaming to those put off by a standard controller. The technology will only improve as higher definition cameras become more affordable. What started as an outrageous experiment is clearly here to stay.

Play it now!

At the time of writing, an enhanced *EyeToy* – featuring increased resolution – has been announced for PlayStation® 3 and is likely to stick to the same format of party games that has made the original such a success. The original *EyeToy* and its add-on titles remain widely available for PlayStation® 2.

EYETOY: PLAY

FINAL FANTASY VII

Publisher: Sony Computer Entertainment Europe/Eidos
Developer: Square Enix Co., Ltd
Platform: PlayStation®, PC
Released: 1997

For many, *FINAL FANTASY VII* marked an introduction to the delights of console role-playing games. And for a very large percentage of them, *FINAL FANTASY VII* will also be the highlight of their gaming career. It's no exaggeration to claim that prior to its release in 1997, nothing like it had been seen before. And to a certain extent, there's been nothing like it since.

As the title suggests, there had been six previous *FINAL FANTASY* titles – but they'd been confined to Nintendo formats, restricted by the limitations of their respective cartridges. The introduction of PlayStation® not only offered Sony a tremendous coup in attracting the seventh in the series away from what had been its spiritual Nintendo home, but

Mega Flare

NAME	BARRIER	HP		MP	LIMIT	TIME
Cloud		899/	930	201		
Barret		647/	993	91		
Aeris		858/	874	187		

I'm glad you're all safe!

afforded the developer a significant storage increase in the form of CD-ROMs. Compact discs offered additional room for visuals and music and could be duplicated cheaply. Square accepted this gratefully. And promptly opted to fill up three separate discs.

They were put to good use. *FINAL FANTASY VII* was streets ahead of anything seen at the time. An epic in every sense, it illustrated in one fell swoop how next generation gaming could for the first time match the original visions of the designers.

A Sony console seemed a strange choice, initially. The trendy PlayStation® adverts aimed at mid-nineties clubbers resulted in the format boasting a different breed of gamers – many utterly unfamiliar with the series. Square and Sony invested a great deal of faith in the game, but a stat-heavy, overblown Japanese role-playing game with turn-based combat still needed to convince in order to become a hit.

But convince it did, selling more than 9 million copies by the end of 2005 on both PlayStation® and, slightly later, PC.

Like all *FINAL FANTASY* games, VII is a story in its own right. A moody mercenary called Cloud Strife is hired by an underground resistance organisation called Avalanche to destroy eight reactors which will ultimately drain the life of the planet. As the game progresses, first through the capital city of Midgar and eventually into the planet itself, Cloud learns his struggle is intricately linked to his past, specifically a shadowy figure named Sephiroth, *FINAL FANTASY VII*'s main protagonist.

"I remember he wrote us 6 or 7 years ago saying that he had a girlfriend. Could that have been you?"

Along the way, Cloud forms a band of warriors, and meets two po[tential] love interests. And it's the subtle [inter]play between these [characters,] conducted throug[hout the] opening CD wh[ich is] possibly respo[nsible] for fans' affinit[y with] the game. Ea[rly on,] Cloud is asked whether he has a [girl]friend. Very few boys who played – su[spect]ing he did, but opting to keep their op[tions] open – will have answered in the [affirma]tive. The cleverly spun plot, with its [gen]uinely outrageous moment a qua[rter of] the way in, generated extreme pa[ssion] among players. Without wishing to [spoil] things, at the start of disc two [Sephi]roth is very much gaming's [most] loathsome character.

Like many of the FINAL FA[NTASY] games, VII's plot draws influ[ence] from many religious, myth[ologi]cal and philoso[phical] themes. It is playe[d] by a cast of stylised characters with outrageous hair, tragic pasts and unfeasibly large weapons. Heartbreaking and foreboding, the narrative progresses to an ambiguous and downbeat conclusion, which was the subject of much debate and interpretation in the intervening years. The fact tht discussion continued for so long after many had finished playing is testament to the plot's quality.

Despite the fresh lick of paint, *FINAL FANTASY VII* plays in a similar style to its predecessors, boasting a mix of exploration, puzzle solving and combat. Whilst the random battles – featuring three characters from the player's

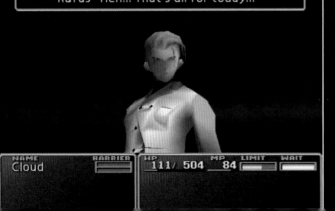

Rufus "Heh... That's all for today..."

NAME: Cloud
BARRIER
HP 111/ 504   MP 84   LIMIT   WAIT

party – could prove occasionally grat-
ing, the grandeur of combat was one
of *FINAL FANTASY VII*'s selling points.
Battle director Yasushi Matsumura
evolved the 'Desperation Move' of
FINAL FANTASY VI – where players
could, under certain conditions, perform
stunning counterattacks – into something
much more spectacular. As players were struck,
a 'Limit Bar' would fill up. When it reached a cer- tain
level, more devastating attacks or special moves could
be launched in retaliation. But it was the summon spells
which really marked a new high in turn-based combat.
Players could summon assistance from magical creatures

resulting in some spectacularly explosive animations, one of which lasted over a minute. Even with repeated viewing, they were never anything less than astonishing.

Driving this along was the celebrated soundtrack, which was commercially released in both a four-disc special edition and two single CD highlights. A number of the game's main themes have been performed by orchestras at various gaming conventions, sending chills down many a fan's spine.

PlayStation® proved such a success for *FINAL FANTASY* that the series has existed more or less exclusively on it ever since. *FINAL FANTASY CRYSTAL CHRONICLES* on GameCube marked an interesting diversion; *FINAL FANTASY TACTICS ADVANCE* on Game Boy Advance was a critically acclaimed strategy game; and the Xbox 360's first massively multiplayer online RPG title *FINAL FANTASY XI* was actually a port of a two-year-old PlayStation® title. Indeed, such was the impact

remember perhaps the greatest game released on PlayStation®, there's little doubt that a full-blown sequel taking players back to the *FINAL FANTASY VII* world so passionately revered would prove Square Enix's most popular game to date.

Play it now!

In the absence of a remake, those wishing to fall for *FINAL FANTASY VII*'s considerable charms could seek out a second-hand copy for PlayStation® although the game is still available as a Platinum release in some territories, and is widely available through specialist stores.

FINAL FANTASY VII © 1997 SQUARE ENIX CO., LTD. All Rights Reserved. FINAL FANTASY is a registered trademark of Square Enix Co., Ltd. CHARACTER DESIGN: TETSUYA NOMURA.

of *FINAL FANTASY VII*, that some of its prequels – if you can call them that – were ported to PlayStation® years later.

But it's *FINAL FANTASY VII* that frequently tops lists of the best games ever, finding favour over its predecessors and subsequent entries in the series. No other *FINAL FANTASY* game has ever boasted such a memorable cast, and it's not unusual to see them cropping up in spin-offs or making cameo appearances in other videogames. A CGI movie was recently released mopping up some of the more inconclusive elements of the original plot. Yet whilst this proved popular with those who

F-Zero™ GX

Publisher: Nintendo
Developer: Sega
Platform: GameCube
Released: 2003

Some people don't like racing games, and if you give it some thought it's easy to understand why. Cars are generally pretty mundane, everyday things, there's not much scope for freedom or imagination in a game where you're just retracing a loop again and again, and the idea of tuning something sounds less like leisure, more like a chore you employ a garage mechanic for. But hey, racing doubters: imagine a racing game where bright coloured aliens fly at a million miles an hour across rollercoasters in space, one which preserves the skill and rhythm and thrill of finding the perfect racing line from 'realistic' racing games, then adds everything that's brilliant about imagination. That's *F-Zero GX*, and that's why you should try it even if you've never considered virtual driving before.

Here's a primer for those unfamiliar with the way a racing game works: you move left, you move right, you go faster, and you try and get to the end as quickly as possible. In *F-Zero*, a game set in the sort of fictional future familiar to anyone who's ever fantasised about flying cars, the courses you race on wind through ludicrously bright environments like endless Chinese dragons. They dip, turn and spin, enclose you in faux-organic tubes that suddenly double back and narrow into angular straights. They twist you like the best amusement park ride ever, all played out at a faster speed than any other racer, and all always under your control.

So it's hardly realistic; what driving purists would sniffily term an 'arcade' racer,

then? Well, possibly; *F-Zero GX* certainly had an arcade counterpart, *F-Zero AX*, and a beautiful pneumatic surround. But the arcade racer tag is almost insulting when weighed against the depth and subtlety of *GX*'s handling. This is not a game you can win by refusing to brake and bouncing off corners. It's more like a serious racing game played in super-fast-forward with elements of a shoot-'em-up. Those come when you're reacting to the position of others. Movement has to take into account the movement of others, which means getting dirty sometimes. This is a game where you have to think on your feet, darting left and right, trying to find a perfect line through clouds of enemies.

There are lots of enemies. Lots and lots, each fleshed out with their own beautiful biography, crazy character design and (improbably) theme song. Each race begins with thirty of them on the track, and a typical finish will see those remaining separated by seconds. A bad crash can have you drop from first to last, which could be frustrating, but when that crash happens it is always your fault. This is not a game that cheats you out of victory; it just teases you with the knowledge that maybe, just maybe you're not quite as good as you hoped.

There is combat in *F-Zero GX*, but not in the

Little known hidden feature: get too good and you have to tow a caravan

often arbitrary, frustrating nature of the *Wipeout* series. It is possible to take out opponents with a swift and hugely satisfying sideswipe, but doing so carries the risk that you'll get your timing wrong and end up losing your rhythm, concentration and the race. Get your timing right, though, and it's possible to accrue both instant speed boosts and crucial advantages in the championship. On later levels this is crucial. It helps a lot on earlier levels too. *F-Zero* is tough.

F-ZERO GX

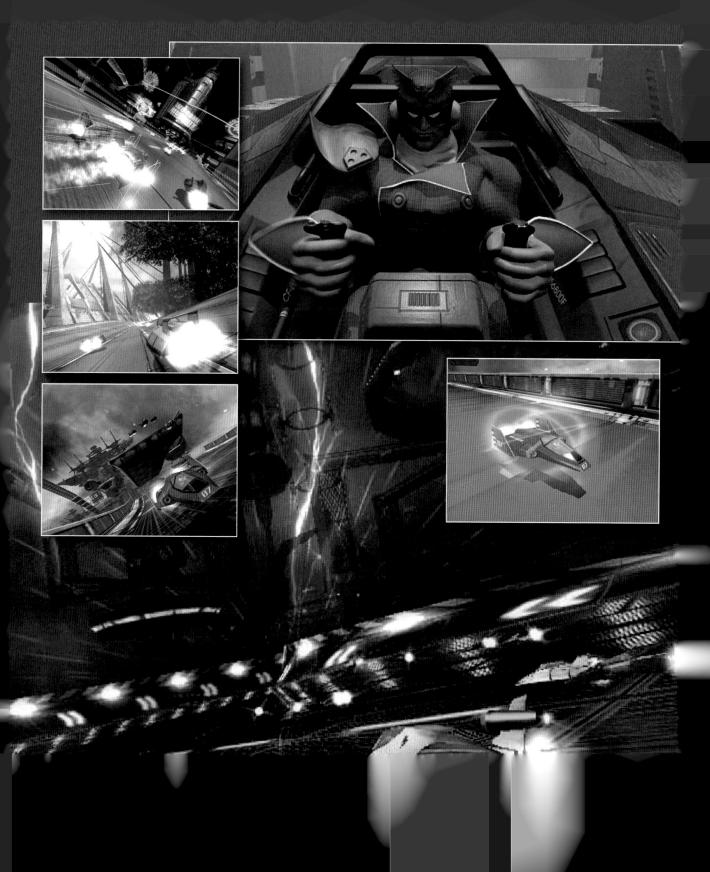

There is plenty of incentive to progress. As you make your way through the game you win credits that you can use to unlock more pilots, ships and courses, and also parts for custom ships that can be built using the simple but highly configurable ship creator. It's easy to lose whole afternoons just tinkering with a design and trialling it on an easy course, shaving thousandths of seconds off lap times and adding a splash of hot pink to your exhaust decals. Looks are as important as speed, obviously.

But the defining characteristic of *F-Zero GX* isn't the beautiful, lucid colourscheme; nor is it the feeling that these fictional tracks are more real than gritty rally circuits, or the thrill you get when you ram another opponent from the track in the crunching combat. It's not the ludicrous number of cars, either, or the brilliant course design. It's all of these things at once, bound by the most crucial of all: the hyper-fast racing, and the feeling you get when you win or lose a race and a championship not by seconds, but by thousandths of seconds. Holding your breath as you speed up to the finish line, neck and neck with your main rival, the heartbeat before the result flashes on screen, and the agony/ecstasy immediately afterwards. That's why *F-Zero GX* isn't just one of the best racing games ever; it's one of the best *videogames* ever, regardless of your genre preference.

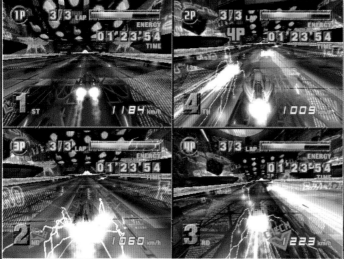

Play it now!

Short of picking up an *F-Zero* arcade machine, which is beautiful but may cost you as much as a small car, the only way to play Sega's latest *F-Zero* game is to get a GameCube and a copy of the game. Both are rapidly disappearing from the shelves, and very soon your best bet might be your local second-hand games store or eBay.

F-Zero™ *GX* © 2003 Nintendo. © AMUSEMENT VISION/SEGA, 2003.

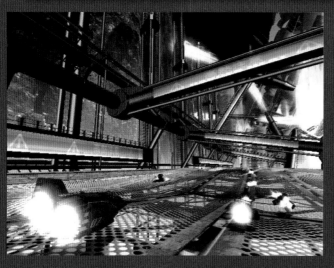

GoldenEye 007™

Publisher: Nintendo
Developer: Rare
Platform: N64
Released: 1997

DAM · FACILITY · RUNWAY · SURFACE · BUNKER
SILO · FRIGATE · SURFACE · BUNKER · STATUE
ARCHIVES · STREETS · DEPOT · TRAIN · JUNGLE
CONTROL · CAVERNS · CRADLE · AZTEC · EGYPTIAN

From the opening strains of that distinctive theme music and that classic gun barrel intro sequence, *GoldenEye 007* captures the very essence of the Bond universe in a way that no other game has. It also manages to incorporate more mayhem than the average John Woo movie, and a multiplayer deathmatch mode which transformed it from yet another movie-licence cash-in into a truly timeless game. It was a perfect combination which propelled the game to sell over 8 million units, making it the best selling N64 game in North America in the process – outselling both *Super Mario 64* and *The Legend of Zelda: Ocarina of Time*.

Ironically, the auguries for *GoldenEye* weren't initially very good. For a start, the game was released two years after the movie upon which it was based. More significantly, and unusually for a console game, it was an FPS – a genre that *Doom* and *Quake* had popularised on the PC but that hadn't yet graced any console with any degree of success. But thanks to the console heritage of its creators, it was heavy on atmosphere and driven by story in a way that those games hadn't

been (*Half-Life*, which was to be similarly story-driven, didn't appear for more than a year after *GoldenEye*).

It created a convincingly authentic environment that was a revelation at the time. Firefights left bullet-holes in walls. Spent bullet cartridges spattered on to the floor. Lights and alarms could be destroyed and windows could be shattered. And individual limbs could be targeted with different degrees of impact (so a head-shot was more lethal than hitting your enemies in their limbs – and would also cause any hat being worn to fall off). But *GoldenEye* also borrowed many features from arcade and console games, such as innocent civilians who had to be kept alive, multiple-mission objectives within the game's individual levels, and a zoomed-in aiming mode.

Indeed, in describing the gestation of the game, its producer Martin Hollis has pointed to the influence of *Virtua Cop* on the design. At the time, developer Rare was a second-party game developer based in the small village of Twycross in England (the filmic opening credits include the Twycross Board of Film Classification certificate – a droll pastiche of the BBFC rating that is shown at the start of movies in the UK). But although Nintendo had raised the possibility of creating a Bond game, there wasn't much interest at Rare. So, as Hollis describes it, he pitched the vague idea of a 3D shooter for the equally vague Nintendo64 (then known as Project Reality). This was then fleshed out into a nine-page design document along the lines of *Virtua Cop*, which would, eventually, transform into one of the best FPS titles ever to have been created.

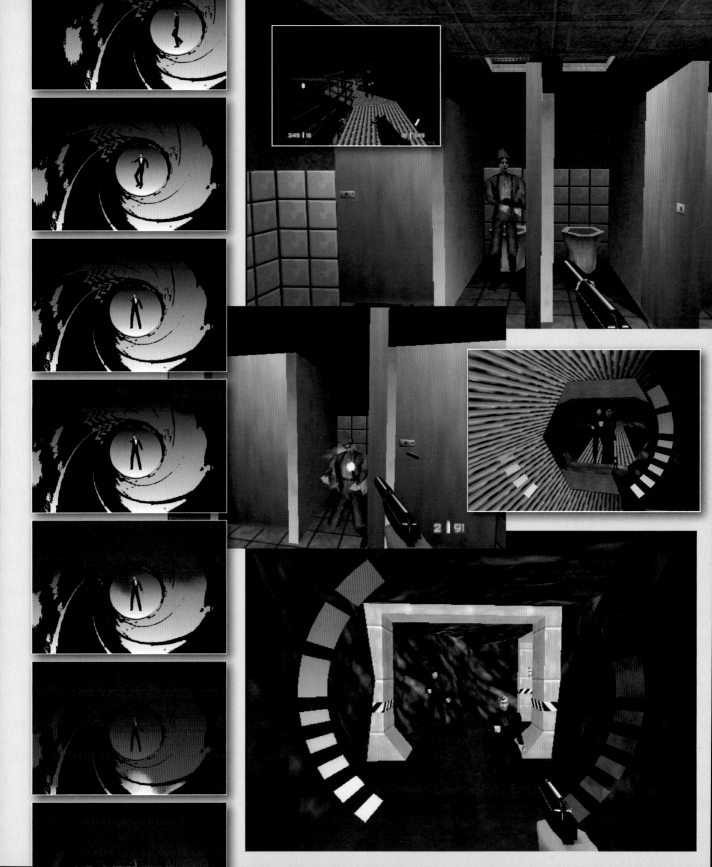

Natalya: This is fun.

One of the key decisions taken by Hollis and his vastly inexperienced team was to feature as many guns and gadgets as they could take from the Bond universe. Weapons like the Walther PPK, AK-47, and PSG-1sniper rifle manifested in the game as the PP7, KF7 Soviet and Sniper Rifle for legal reasons, but were all totally convincing. Some pistols and machine-guns could be wielded in pairs and the extravagant zoom function of the sniper rifle helped establish the weapon as a mainstay of the genre – partly because it was so enormously satisfying. Gadgets like the watch laser, covert modem, key analyser and trusty camera were chosen and then incorporated into the game's levels, creating many of the game's objectives, and some amazingly memorable moments .

The movie was mined exhaustively, with the development team visiting many of the movie's sets. Like the film, the game opens up on the Byelomorye dam, from which Bond performs a death-defying bungee jump. Later levels include a dash along a runway to reach a plane; icy wastes, underground bunkers, the interior of a moving train and a recreation of the movie's tank chase and climactic showdown at The Cradle. Along the way, there is a huge variety of playing styles, from snow-based sniping and infiltration, to balls-out gunfights in underground bunkers.

Two additional levels could also be unlocked, one based on *Moonraker* and featuring Bond's metal-mouthed nemesis Jaws; the other a montage of *The Man With the Golden Gun*, *The Spy Who Loved Me* and *Live and Let Die*. What tied these to the game's other levels, is that they were all extremely non-linear, giving players a choice of different routes and posing the decision whether to use stealth or action. In addition, each of the game's three difficulty settings introduced a different set of objectives, bestowing an unusually rewarding replay value.

But for all its Bondness, *GoldenEye* wouldn't have been such an enormous hit were it not for the inclusion of a ground-breaking multiplayer mode. Created almost as an afterthought by Steve Ellis, it was a crucial factor in the game's success. Playable by up to four players, across 11 arenas, it featured a comprehensive variety of game types, from regular deathmatches to a one-hit-kill mode (*Licensed to Kill*) and a mode based around the Golden Gun. Players could choose from an enormous number of character models, including classic Bond characters such as Oddjob and Jaws, and the likenesses of various Rare employees (such as David Doak, credited in the manual for 'Original Screenplay', who appears in the single-player game as a double agent). It remained the definitive multiplayer experience on consoles until they went online.

GoldenEye itself remained the definitive Bond game, and, for a long time, the definitive console FPS. Rare's spiritual sequel, *Perfect Dark*, probably came the closest to matching *GoldenEye*'s excellence, but crucially it lacked the atmosphere and coherence of the Bond universe, and it strained the N64 beyond its technical ability. And so it wasn't for another four years, till the arrival of *Halo* on a next generation console, that another title could hold a candle to Hollis's superb creation. But that's another story …

Play it now!

Publishing powerhouse Electronic Arts recently relaunched the *GoldenEye* brand when it released *GoldenEye: Rogue Agent* for PlayStation® 2, Xbox and GameCube. Don't be fooled though – it's got absolutely nothing in common with the original *GoldenEye* except the name, and it's probably best avoided. Sadly then, the only way to play *GoldenEye* in its original incarnation is to get hold of a second-hand Nintendo64 and a copy of the original game – although there are various projects online, such as *GoldenEye Source*, which aim to recreate the levels and characters from Rare's masterwork within current FPS titles, such as Valve's *Half-Life 2*.

Grand Theft Auto III

Publisher: Rockstar Games, Inc.
Developer: DMA Design
Platform: PlayStation®, PC (2002), Xbox (2003)
Released: 2001

Every gamer has one. Whether it's something as inconsequential as observing a rainbow over Liberty City for the first time, or something as significant as figuring out an unorthodox solution to a tricky mission – there's a moment in *Grand Theft Auto III* where everything just falls into place. And from that point on, traditional, linear gaming seems so, well, last generation.

Few games have successfully survived the transition from two to three dimensions. The introduction of the 32-bit consoles proved the undoing of hugely successful 16-bit development teams as they struggled to adapt to the demands of a new generation of technology. Games which thrilled as sprite-based outings suddenly became broken polygonal

Charity touts were less of a problem these days

titles; witness Sensible Soccer's first 3D outing after years of dominating the two-dimensional genre. Actually, don't – it's best left forgotten.

GTA, however, has thrived since the introduction of an additional dimension, thanks mainly to the foundations laid down right back in the first game, released for PlayStation® and PC. Sure, each subsequent iteration adds more and more layers, but overall the series has stuck rigidly to the principles founded by DMA Design (later to become Rockstar North) right back in 1998.

Grand Theft Auto offered players a simple premise: explore a city, commit crimes for money and avoid the police. The original game boasted three distinct play areas: Liberty City, Vice City and San Andreas, each based on approximations of real American conurbations. Even the series' trademark in-car radio made an early if primitive appearance. If it all sounds

peers. Players were given complete freedom to use whatever tools were at hand in order to complete missions. If everything was proving a little too tough, they could complete additional side-missions and tasks in order to accrue more money and weapons.

GTA is the first prominent example of what would subsequently become known as 'sandbox' gaming. Whilst games such as *Elite* and *Sim City* had offered an open-ended style of play, none had combined this with an overlying story arc or goal. *GTA* was a linear game with non-linear mechanics. As such, it presented a vision of the future which was as exciting as it was uncompromising.

GTA II and GTA London evolved the sandbox premise, but it was *GTA III* which really established the series. Released in 2001 for PlayStation® 2, it would have been more appropriately named had a 'D' been suffixed to indicate the extra dimension This was everything *GTA* had offered before, but in a beautifully rendered, fully 3D city. Day and night cycles, distinct city districts, a fully-developed cast of characters – for the first time, the dream of playing in a virtual world was close to being fulfilled. *GTA III* offered a series of building bricks. How they were used was left entirely to the player.

familiar, it certainly won't look it – the game was mainly sprite-based, running in two rather than three dimensions.

Whilst it wouldn't turn heads with its visuals, it was the open-ended style of play which really distanced *GTA* from its

GRAND THEFT AUTO 3

Grand Theft Auto San Andreas:
welcome to Vinewood.

The game begins with the player being transferred to prison, following an unsuccessful bank robbery during which he's stitched up by his girlfriend. En route to the jail, the van is attacked, allowing him to escape and begin finding work for local gang bosses. At the start of *GTA III*, the player's character – interestingly, never given a name – is a petty hoodlum. By the end of the game, he's taken out several crime bosses himself and wreaked revenge upon his treacherous ex-girlfriend. It's quite a ride.

As in previous games, car-jacking and crime formed the central gameplay components – but missions could be accepted at any time, and tackled in any way. Talk to anyone who's played *GTA III* and they'll all have different solutions to common missions; to many, it's the same name, but a different game. And that was its fundamental beauty.

Despite the controversy caused by the game's release, *GTA III* did not encourage blatant lawlessness. A finely balanced risk cause and effect system is in play, making the game more difficult if players needlessly commit crimes. Doing so attracts the attention of the game's police force, who employ all manner of tactics to bring players to justice. Depending on the level of the crime, players soon find themselves being rammed off the road by a chasing pack of police cars, or even forced off the road with roadblocks or tyre-slashing 'stingers'. At moments of utter mayhem, helicopters also give chase. Only by collecting police 'bribes' or re-painting the getaway car can players survive without being killed or sent to jail. There's your lesson for you, kids. Crime doesn't pay. Although it is often fun.

Of course, the controversy helped, but *GTA* didn't become the most successful game of 2001 just because it was a bit naughty. No, *GTA III* was one of the most solid games of its time, mainly because the foundations had been tested in the previous titles. Whilst full games in their own right, there's no doubt *GTA III* benefited from the prototyping of its two-dimensional predecessors.

The *GTA* team returned to their original game for titular inspiration a year later. *Vice City* took place before the events in *GTA III*, moving the action to a sun-drenched city inspired by Miami, and coating it in a wonderful 80s-inspired aura, from the staggering array of licensed tunes to the fashions. The game refined the mechanics of *GTA III* whilst introducing additional diversions in the form of property ownership and associated side missions. Rockstar didn't fix what wasn't broken, and as such *GTA: Vice City* outperformed *GTA III*. It was the most popular game of 2002 – *GTA III* was second – and remains, to this date, the most successful PlayStation® 2 game in America, ever.

Grand Theft Auto San Andreas was released for home consoles and PC in 2004, offering character customisation for the first time in the series. It is also widely credited as being the last in the *GTA III* 'trilogy' – despite the release of spin-offs such as *Liberty City Stories* on PSP™ in 2005.

Where the series heads next remains to be seen. But right here, right now, it's at the very top of its game. Sure, Lara Croft or *Halo*'s Master Chief would disagree, but no other title can command as much attention – both wanted and unwanted – as Rockstar's ground-breaking series.

Relish the lush, sun-drenched hues of **Grand Theft Auto: Vice City**

Play it now!

GTA III is available on both PlayStation® 2 and Xbox – either on its own or as part of value bundles. *Liberty City Stories* recreates *GTA III*'s world admirably on PSP™ – though the missions differ, it's essentially the same game.

Grand Theft Auto III © 2003 Take Two Interactive Software Europe Ltd. All Rights Reserved.

Gran Turismo 4

Publisher: Sony Computer Entertainment
Developer: Polyphony Digital
Platform: PlayStation® 2
Released: 2004

Pokémon *for petrolheads:*
GT4 *contains over 700 cars*

Imagine a world in which the closest videogame approximation to driving was a flickering rendition of some blocky white road posts to outline the road ahead. Did the creators of Atari's *Night Driver*, in 1976, ever imagine a world in which you could simply switch on a videogame console and roar round the Nürburgring, experiencing the throaty howl of a highly tuned engine, and the sunlight strobing behind the tree tops with such lifelike exactness that you can almost smell the petrol? Imagine a world without *Gran Turismo*.

Before *Gran Turismo*, racing games were either quick-fix arcade affairs featuring caricatured handling, or pedantically accurate Formula One sims. *GT* straddled this divide, encompassing the whole spectrum of driving game experiences, revitalising the genre and selling millions of copies in the process (the original *Gran Turismo* was the best selling game on PSone). *Gran Turismo 4* is the pinnacle of the series so far – presenting an evolution of all its defining hallmarks.

The first thing you notice about it is the almost overwhelming scale of the game. The series was once memorably described as *Pokémon* for petrolheads, and it's a pretty astute observation: *GT4* features over 700 real world cars, 80 car manufacturers and over 50 racetracks. You can race around circuits such as the Nürburgring, and Le Mans, and landmarks like Times Square and the drag strip in Las Vegas. You can test drive Audis, Alfa Romeos, Aston Martins, Chevrolets, Chryslers, Fords, Mercedes, Mitsubishis, Toyotas, BMWs and beyond. Cars cater to the needs of boy racers, classic collectors, and even include curios such as the Nissan GT-R Concept.

Like previous versions of *Gran Turismo*, an arcade mode provides an accessible option to sample this comprehensive vehicle selection, as well as an opportunity to take on friends in split-screen or local network multiplayer mode. *GT4* also introduces a couple of new modes: B-spec racing, in which players choose race tactics for an AI racer, and Photo Travel Mode, in which players can take photos. But the real substance of the game is to be found in the main career mode, in which players start by picking up a cheap motor, pass driving tests, enter (an inordinate number of) competitions, and

spend their winnings tuning current vehicles or buying new ones, till they've raced around the world and picked up every vehicle in the game.

As much as the game is about collecting all the cars though, it's also about the authenticity of the driving experience. The original game came with a driving manual explaining when to brake for corners and how to accelerate out of them, and according to Polyphony a professional driver's lap times on GT4's in-game Nürburgring Nordschleife were within 2% of their real life equivalents.

But it's not just professional drivers who benefit from a level of realism that incorporates aerodynamic spoilers to increase downforce, tyre wear, oil changes, and a physics model that differentiates between front-, rear-, and four-wheel drive (in contrast to the uniformly brick-like dynamics of pre-Gran Turismo racers). An unexpected, and perhaps ironic, upshot of what might be considered an off-putting degree of authenticity is that the original GT was unusually appealing to mainstream gamers. For the first time, cars behaved as they do in real life, so there was no need to get to grips with unlikely manoeuvres like powerslides or bunny hops. Instead, there was just the exhilaration of a satisfying engine roar and taking bends at high speed in tuned racers.

Another unexpected upshot of Gran Turismo's success was its impact on car showrooms around the world.

Anecdotal evidence suggested that the game sparked a renewed interest in real-life versions of cars that were difficult to unlock in the game, and in the US, the game paved the way for an upsurge of interest in Japanese imports such as the Subaru Impreza WRX and Nissan Skyline, and European marques like Aston Martin and Alfa Romeo. These circumstantial stories were given credence when Sony released two demo discs of GT4 before its release. The first featured the Toyota Prius and the Toyota MTRC concept car, on the Fuji Speedway 90s and Grand Canyon circuits, and was used by Toyota to promote the marketing brochure for the 2004 Prius. The second featured all four models of BMW's 1-series, and three tracks.

The real-world significance of Gran Turismo is testament to its in-game excellence. Sure, you can criticise the AI of other drivers, or the lack of car damage modelling, but GT is a game in which you compete with the course and not other racers. The original Gran Turismo set a benchmark for other driving games to follow and spawned a wave of imitators; none has succeeded to quite the same extent as Gran Turismo 4 – until the next game in the series arrives on PlayStation® 3.

Play it now!

Gran Turismo 4 is available now, for the PlayStation® 2 – as is Tourist Trophy, a motorcycle racing game created by the same development team, based on the same underlying physics engine as GT4.

Guitar Hero

Publisher: RedOctane
Developer: Harmonix Music Systems
Platform: PlayStation® 2
Released: 2005 US, 2006 Europe

Guitar Hero is a modern-day gaming phenomenon, proof positive that in this day of multi-million-pound development budgets and saturated marketing, it's possible to reap huge rewards from good old-fashioned innovation and the balls to pursue a single vision. Oh, and a plastic guitar.

Until November 2005, RedOctane was a relatively unknown US publisher which had little focus in the games industry. In 1999, the firm launched itself as the world's first online games rental service – years before there was any real market. From 2001 to 2004, RedOctane concentrated on developing and selling dance mats; in the summer of 2005 it published a PlayStation® 2 dance game In The Groove, to limited success. After six years in the interactive entertainment industry, RedOctane remained a company few in the business could name.

That all changed with Guitar Hero – a title fuelled by the desire to create a game which offered players the sensation of being an sweatband-wearing, greasy-haired, guitar-wielding rock god.

Developed by Harmonix, a developer which had cut its rhythm-action teeth on Amplitude and Frequency, on screen Guitar Hero breaks little ground. Similar to more traditional rhythm action games such as Dancing Stage, coloured icons tumble down the screen on a virtual fret-board, with players hitting corresponding buttons in time with the music. Miss too many, the crowd will begin to moan. Continue to perform badly, and it's game over. The more notes hit consecutively, the higher the score – with multipliers and 'star power' playing important parts. Special

sustains need to be held down for longer, and the introduction of the analogue 'whammy' at these points results in a higher score.

So far, so ordinary – this could be a description of almost any other rhythm action game. But Guitar Hero is different in two vital areas: the choice of music, and the input device.

What a jolly ditty. And your fingering is exemplary

The 30 licensed songs hail from a pool of the world's greatest rock tracks. Some contemporary singles are here – Franz Ferdinand's *Take Me Out*, Queens of the Stone Age's *No-One Knows* and Sum 41's *Fat Lip* would be the most recognisable to a typical PlayStation® owner. Whilst these songs are fun, it's the rock classics such as *More Than A Feeling*, *I Wanna Be Sedated*, *Ziggy Stardust* and, of course, *Ace of Spades* which really shine. 17 additional tracks can be unlocked throughout the game's various modes, though these hail from up and coming bands so aren't necessarily a key selling point.

The peripheral included in the package certainly is, though. A three-quarter replica of the classic Gibson SG guitar, it's a masterpiece of modern games engineering, featuring five fret buttons, a strum bar and a working whammy lever. The guitar even includes a tilt sensor which recognises when it's being played vertically – gaining additional points at key moments in the game.

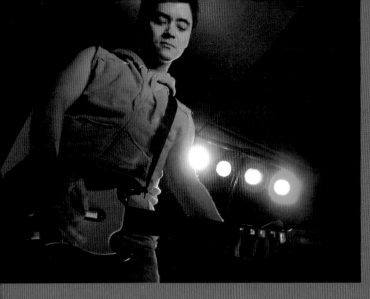

few minutes. Tales abound of PlayStation® owners graduating to real Gibsons thanks to their experience with a three-quarter replica, so convincing is the marriage of code and peripheral in *Guitar Hero*.

An additional guitar can be hooked up for multiplayer sessions, and the most spectacular scores are recorded for posterity in graffiti above the in-game urinal. Yes, this really is rock and roll – and we like it.

The game itself was written in nine short months, following the construction of a successful SG controller prototype. In a world dominated by licences, and ever-conscious of cost, a game requiring a dedicated peripheral from an unknown publisher really shouldn't succeed. But be thankful that RedOctane's single-mindedness in bringing the game to market paid off. Whilst sequels and add-ons for the Gibson SG controller are in the works, one can presume that *Guitar Hero* is only the start – subsequent instruments are rumoured to be in development.

For a medium designed to entertain, modern games can be increasingly po-faced. For that and so many other reasons, *Guitar Hero* is a breath of fresh air, designed not just to make the player enjoy an unparalleled gaming experience – but everyone else watching, too.

Crucially, the psychology of guitar playing is replicated perfectly. Just by slinging the SG over your shoulders, you immediately feel like a rock god. The legs move slightly further apart – maybe the strap is adjusted to position the guitar closer to the knees. The left hand naturally assumes a position on the fretboard, the right hovering over the strum bar. And then you play. Boy, do you play.

Perfectly choreographed to mimic the hand movements on a real guitar – low notes are played at the end of the guitar, high notes towards the body – *Guitar Heroes* really do feel as if they're making the music. Even legitimate guitar techniques can be employed, so those who know their hammer-ons from their hammer-offs will be at an instant advantage. But even if you couldn't strum a note before, you'll be convinced you can after a

Play it now!

RedOctane is seeking to establish the Gibson SG controller as a format in its own right. The firm has promised that any sequels and add-ons will work with the original *Guitar Hero* guitar, ensuring that there's never a bad time to buy a game from the series. *Guitar Hero 2* is scheduled for release during late 2006 – but the best bet is to pick up the original title now and enjoy sequels and add-ons as software-only purchases.

Half-Life

Publisher: Havas Interactive
Developer: Valve, LLC
Platform: PC
Released: 2001

Who'd have thought a bespectacled, bearded, ginger-haired scientist could become one of the most popular gaming heroes of all time? Quite frankly, as icons go, Gordon Freeman is probably up there with your geography teacher or an embarrassing uncle. But little about *Half-Life* or its hero is conventional. For starters, it was developer Valve's first ever game.

So it's no surprise that *Half-Life* broke all the rules. Ever since iD Software's *Wolfenstein 3D* popularised the genre, first-person shooters typically remained true to their name: players shot things in games presented in a first-person perspective. Plot exposition was limited to text screens at first, with cut-scenes coming later – but both completely shattered any illusions of immersion. Monsters became bigger, environments less brown – but the games themselves stuck rigidly to the same mechanic. Shoot things, open doors, operate platforms, find keys, move on.

Right from the subdued opening to *Half-Life*, however, it is obvious this is different. The introduction takes place in-game itself as players journey on a monorail to the heart of the Black Mesa Research Facility. No hand-holding tutorials, no menu screens – the first few minutes are spent in awe, as the characters within the complex continue their day-to-day chores. It's a true sight to behold: If the technology had existed at the time, you can be sure Valve would have included a routine to leave greasy forehead marks on the inside of the monorail, as players admired everything on display during this most impressive preface.

For Gordon Freeman, though, this is just supposed to be an ordinary day. The monorail introduction actually represents his commute to work. The opening level – the trek to his

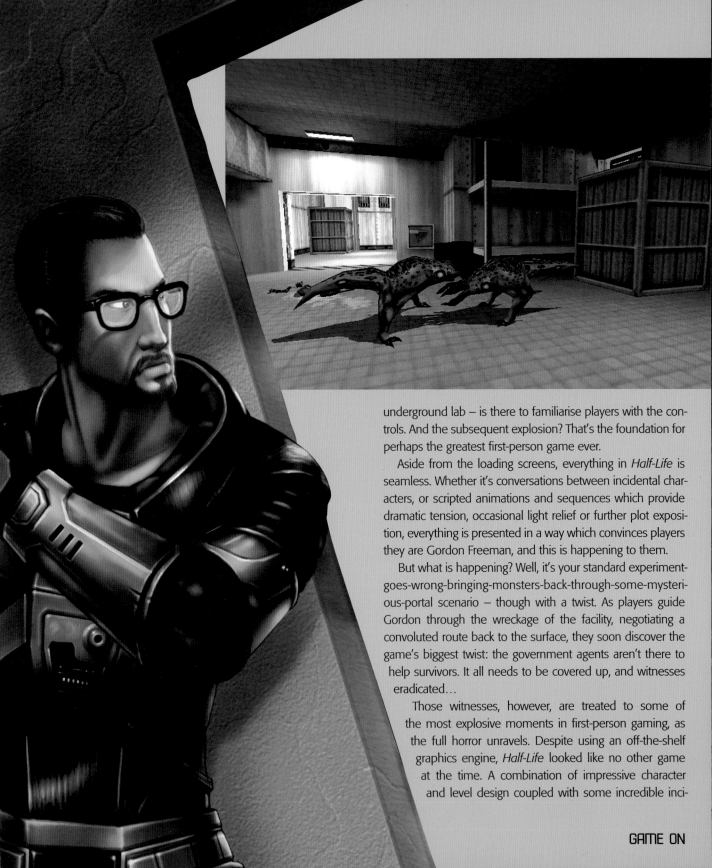

underground lab – is there to familiarise players with the controls. And the subsequent explosion? That's the foundation for perhaps the greatest first-person game ever.

Aside from the loading screens, everything in *Half-Life* is seamless. Whether it's conversations between incidental characters, or scripted animations and sequences which provide dramatic tension, occasional light relief or further plot exposition, everything is presented in a way which convinces players they are Gordon Freeman, and this is happening to them.

But what is happening? Well, it's your standard experiment-goes-wrong-bringing-monsters-back-through-some-mysterious-portal scenario – though with a twist. As players guide Gordon through the wreckage of the facility, negotiating a convoluted route back to the surface, they soon discover the game's biggest twist: the government agents aren't there to help survivors. It all needs to be covered up, and witnesses eradicated…

Those witnesses, however, are treated to some of the most explosive moments in first-person gaming, as the full horror unravels. Despite using an off-the-shelf graphics engine, *Half-Life* looked like no other game at the time. A combination of impressive character and level design coupled with some incredible inci-

the highly anticipated sequel, *Half-Life 2*, was released in 2004, to similar critical reception. But it's the original which remains the best selling PC game in the genre to date – undoubtedly kept alive through its numerous appearances at the top of annual 'best game ever' charts, word of mouth and healthy mod scene. Additional scenarios and levels have been released over the years, either filling in gaps in the story, or telling it again from another point of view – but good as these are, they rarely reach the same giddy heights as the original.

Whilst all these additions obviously help keep *Half-Life* alive, the original adventure remains by far the best. It's a shame it's impossible to play a game for the first time once again.

dental detail made Black Mesa and its surroundings as beautiful as they were deadly. Fights were tough: sophisticated artificial intelligence could genuinely confound even the genre's most experienced players. As the game careered through set-piece after set-piece, players encountered battles and moments of such euphoric high tension that even the somewhat disappointing ending could not significantly dent.

The game was released in an enhanced form on Play-Station® 2 in 2001, complete with an additional expansion pack offering head to head and co-op play. Dreamcast and Macintosh versions were also completed but never released – the Sega port clearly suffered because of the demise of the format, but the Macintosh release reportedly was not compatible with the PC multiplayer components.

After a significant amount of hype at the industry's various trade shows,

Halo: Combat Evolved

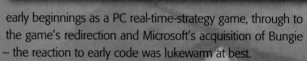

Publisher: Microsoft Game Studios
Developer: Bungie Studios
Platform: Xbox, PC
Released: 2001

How pivotal to the Xbox's success was *Halo*? Big question, long answer: when Microsoft were preparing to launch the original Xbox in 2001, many people were already writing them off as a serious challenger to Sony's dominance. They could have thrown as much money at the project as they wanted, but ultimately it would be the games that were the machine's selling points, and early rumours had the Xbox lineup as dull and uninspired. Microsoft's only real defence? *Halo*. But launch titles are always weak, and despite being sought after for years previously – from its early beginnings as a PC real-time-strategy game, through to the game's redirection and Microsoft's acquisition of Bungie – the reaction to early code was lukewarm at best.

First things first. *Halo* is a first person shooter. On the surface it is every bit as sophisticated as that description suggests: you view the world through the eyes of the protagonist, and you shoot things. But while *Halo* might be violent, it is anything but mindless. Certainly the most intelligently designed FPS to ever make its debut on a console, and possibly the smartest ever, Halo proves that the gameplay in a shooter can carry as much impact as the gunplay.

You take the role of Master Chief, a killing machine of the future defrosted to help humanity fight a losing battle against The Covenant, a race of ruthless, quasi-religious aliens. You're thrown into battle almost as soon as you've come out of hibernation, the aliens boarding your cruiser and storming the bridge, but the fun really starts when your escape pod crashes on the ringworld of the title. Suddenly what appeared to be a corridor shoot-'em-up opens out into a lush, green planet, wide spaces provoking agoraphobia and giving you back something so many FPSs lack: space and freedom.

Halo's most import innovations are twofold. First, throughout the adventure you're only allowed to hold two weapons at any time. Since the combat experience changes with whatever weapon you choose to take, and since ammo is often very limited, each weapon you find on the floor becomes a fork in the road. Pick up the machine-gun or stick with the sniper rifle, even though you've only five bullets left? Take a plasma rifle that you're uncomfortable using to replace the shotgun which doesn't seem very effective right now? Decisions like those litter the game.

Secondly, Master Chief has a shield which will recharge if he avoids taking fire for a few seconds. For years before *Halo*, first person shooters followed a predictable pattern of damage

As a young cyborg, Master Chief actually wanted to be a train driver

and repair. The player would enter a battle, lose some health, seek out one of hundreds of health kits ludicrously scattered around the game world, then battle some more and lose some more health, and so on. Combat in *Halo* is a much smarter experience; as soon as you're in a fight you're looking for cover. Under non-stop fire from the enemy, you don't just hold your breath for the next health recharge. You use the environment to help you.

Critics have decried those environments as repetitive, which they undoubtedly are, and the enemy AI as built from elementary routines, just producing smoke and mirrors for the player to lose themselves in. But that doesn't matter, because when you play *Halo* you *are* lost. Regardless of how their intelligence has been constructed, it's entirely about the experience: every enemy you're fighting against feels like it's thinking for itself, feels smart and confident and potentially deadly, and that's what puts the game in the upper echelons of the genre.

What elevates it still further into the running for best first person shooter ever is the way that AI interacts with itself, simple rules cascading down through the game to ensure the player rarely encounters exactly the same situation twice. Every single battle in *Halo* is a short story you write yourself. There are very few set-pieces throughout the whole adventure; those scripted Oh-My-God moments that made *Half-Life* arrive here unplanned.

If you're already sold on the game, go play it now, because this paragraph contains spoilers. Midway through the game you're introduced to a new type of enemy: The Flood, a parasitic, zombie-style race whose artificial intelligence is limited to heading straight for you and shooting. But The Flood don't like The Covenant either, and all of a sudden the conflict splits

Once again, this means the quickload gameplay so prevalent in previous first person shooters, where the player learns the patterns of the enemy, dies in the process but then loads a saved game from a few minutes previously and manages to defeat the enemy with precognitive combat, is largely absent here. Battles unfold in different ways on every reload. There's no point in remembering which direction an enemy runs in because it's always different.

Does it help that the enemy is quite so fugly?

three ways, with beings on each side trying to kill each other while doing their best to stay alive. There are points in *Halo* when you can step back and watch from a distance as The Covenant and The Flood tear each other to shreds. And there are other points when both sides are coming for you and there's nothing you can do except duck for cover and fight back.

HALO: COMBAT EVOLVED

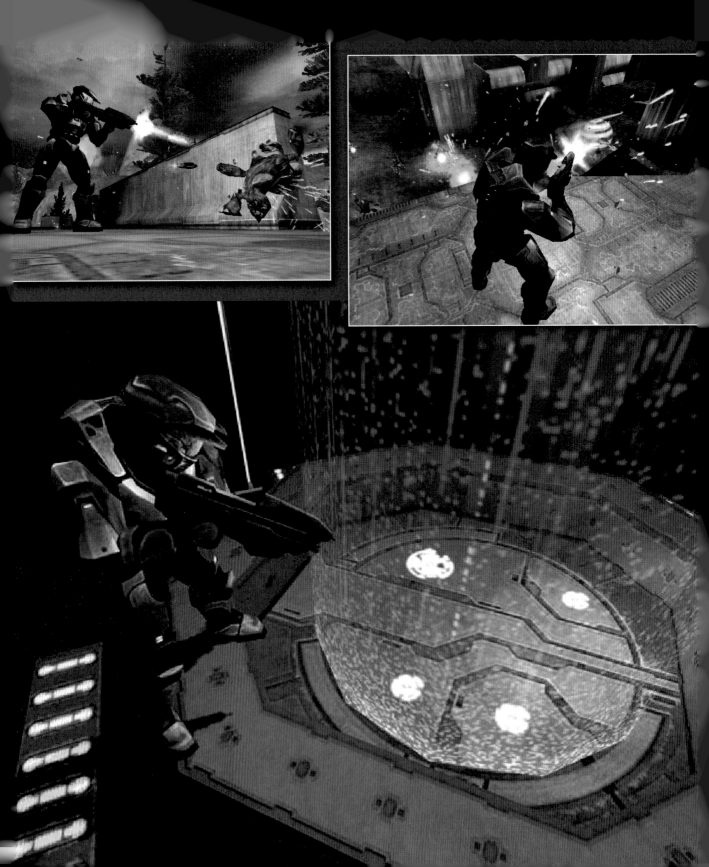

So complaints about *Halo*'s environmental structures repeating throughout the adventure are utterly redundant. It would not make one jot of difference to the game if the places where you have the battles underwent a quick texture and lighting change, because the combat – the focus of the game, as this is a first person shooter, not a first person architectural adventure – changes throughout.

For those who want to look beyond the shooting: the story is compulsive and well told, the characters believable and nicely acted, the visuals sweet and effective. There are excellent multiplayer modes too, particularly for those with the resources and patience to link together two Xboxes; eight player wars across the bigger maps are as fun as you'd imagine digital paintball to be. But the main reason people bought the game, and the Xbox, was *Halo*. A rarely paralleled critical reception heralded

Halo's arrival, and so the Xbox arrived on the crest of this wave. Five years on, and the wave has long since crested, but *Halo* remains the definitive title for Microsoft's first machine. Short answer: You don't get much more pivotal than that.

Play it now!

Halo is widely available for the Xbox, and will run on the Xbox 360 too. *Halo 2* excels in multiplayer, but the original is still the best for those who want a single-player experience.

Halo: Combat Evolved images reprinted with permission from Microsoft Corporation.

Ico™

Publisher: Sony Computer Entertainment
Developer: SCEI/Fumito Ueda
Platform: PlayStation® 2
Released: 2001

Ico™ is an understated, elegantly minimalist masterpiece. It packs more action, emotion and artistry into its relatively brief duration than most other games do in twenty hours or more. Its restrained narrative is more engaging; its disembodied, dream-like setting is more compelling; and the grim fairytale at its heart is more poignant than all those bloated videogame epics that mistake quantity for quality.

Its beautiful box artwork was designed after the style of an early twentieth century surrealist painter called Giorgio de Chirico. It provides a pretty good hint of what's to come, by depicting a small figure urgently leading another across an insubstantial sun-bleached landscape. The game itself features a similarly over-exposed visual motif, creating some of the most stylistically attractive sights in videogame history as the game relates the simple, yet powerfully resonant story of a boy who is taken to be sacrificed, but who is destined to deliver a princess from imprisonment.

The game's minimalist hue extends across its every aspect. Featuring very little music, and dispensing with the voice-over exposition that characterises most other games, its narrative is pared back to the barest of bones: it's boy meets girl. The boy in question, the Ico of the title, is a small boy who was born with horns and who is thus fated to be sacrificed by his people. The game commences as he is being taken to his execution, by entombment within a sarcophagus located inside a mysterious castle. But a freak tremor frees him to explore the castle, which is where the player takes over. It's not long before he finds the girl in question, the delicate and elfin Yorda. It's then up to the player to take over their plight, and their attempts to flee in the face of a metaphysical darkness within the castle that prevents their escape.

Continuing the game's stripped-back style, the castle itself is austere, taking its inspiration from a rich variety of sources outside the world of videogames. Like Mervyn Peake's classic fantasy epic

The daunting interior of the game's castle setting casts a long shadow

It's an architectural space that is unlike anything to be found in any other videogame

novel *Gormenghast*, it imposes its own Gothic character on the game, and interacting with it defines a large part of the game. It's an architectural space that is unlike anything to be found in any other videogame, and for the closest comparison to the castle's colossal expanses and apparently purposeless machinery, you'd probably have to look to the eighteenth century artist Giovanni Battista Piranesi and his elaborately detailed sketches of *Imaginary Prisons*.

The majority of the game sees players exploring these cavernously spartan chambers, investigating its occasional courtyards and quadrangles, and discovering vast, towering edifices and subterranean coves and caves. Sporadic, breathtaking glimpses of the sun-scorched lands beyond the castle grounds serve only to heighten its sense of confinement and isolation, and howling winds and rushing waters peter out and fade away as Ico and Yorda advance deeper into the castle's interior.

It's Ico's duty to take the helpless Yorda by the hand to steer her through these epic constructions: running, jumping, climbing, pushing blocks and pulling

levers to eliminate any obstacles to her progress. But if Yorda is left alone for too long while Ico searches for a solution to a puzzle, she will come under attack from the castle's inhabitants: shadowy phantom spectres who emerge out of the ground itself to pull her back down with them. The game's unusually bare approach then extends even to the game's combat interface, which features none of the clutter normally associated with videogames: so there's no inventory screen, no health meter, and no power bar.

The game's aesthetic frugality results from a conscious design decision taken by the game's creator, Fumito Ueda, when he conceived of a project that was initially intended for the original PlayStation®. As he has since explained, he wanted to explore this theme of boy-meets-girl because of its universality, and he decided upon its visual representation by hand holding from the outset. Several early concepts arising out of these ideas were considered before their eventual rejection, including a scenario featuring a servant boy and girl confined within a castle, and a scenario which would have seen the pair escaping or surviving in a town or desert island. Other intriguing differences between the original design and the eventual game include a more complex combat system and the fact that it was originally to be the female character that was to have horns.

When the game went into full production, it was with several goals: to adopt a different approach to that of other games; to distinguish its 3D graphics by making them stylistic, rather than photorealistic; to try to create a sense of reality through emotional connection rather than visual accuracy; and, above all, to reduce the game in scale and complexity in order to increase the 'density' of the game world. By concentrating on just the castle and its grounds, on just the two protagonists and on just one type of enemy, Ueda hoped to make these elements more convincing, and reduce the likelihood of any jarring discontinuities interrupting the player's suspension of disbelief. But it wasn't until the project was switched to PlayStation® 2 at the end of 1999 that it could be completed without compromising these goals.

This refusal to compromise is utterly vindicated by the finished game. Out of Ueda's delicate approach is hewn an unyielding solidity. The castle is certainly the most resolutely convincing structure in any videogame. More importantly, there's an emotional substantiality born of the game design. By forcing the player to care for Yorda's survival, the game intensifies the emotional connection between Yorda and Ico, massively enhancing the dramatic scope of the game, and lifting the quality of the narrative from the banal to the sublime. It reaches its surprising conclusion with an inspiringly spectacular climactic boss battle that, in its brevity, redefines the usually tedious test of a gamer's patience.

When the game does reach its end, it leaves a yawning chasm in its wake that's almost as painful as a kick to the stomach. When the game is switched off it leaves behind more questions than answers, and a yearning to find out more about the fate of its two lead characters. It leaves behind a gap that's difficult to fill – which is wholly surprising, but superbly satisfying in a videogame.

Play it now!

Ico™ met more critical acclaim upon its release than it did commercial success, but it sold 650,000 copies across the world which was enough to spawn a spiritual successor called *Shadow of the Colossus*™ that, ironically, re-ignited interest in *Ico*™. Consequently, gamers in Europe benefited from a re-release, so the game is available to play now on PlayStation® 2.

Jak and Daxter: The Precursor Legacy™

Publisher: Sony Computer Entertainment
Developer: Naughty Dog
Platform: PlayStation® 2
Released: 2001

Jak and Daxter marks the point at which its developer Naughty Dog went off the rails. It marks the point at which the company opened up the platform genre from the linear, disconnected levels to be found in its previous PlayStation® games to create a seamlessly integrated game world, complete with all the features that made its previous games so popular. So that's all the crates you could dream of smashing; all the logs you could ever want to jump over; more mine carts than you could ever ride; the obligatory lava worlds; and the oddest, most wisecrackingest couple of protagonists that you could possibly hope to meet. Oh, and a mysterious substance called Eco…

If you owned a PlayStation® in the 1990s there was really only one platform game series that could compete with the likes of *Super Mario 64* and *Banjo Kazooie* on the N64: Naughty Dog's *Crash Bandicoot*. Each game in the series saw players jumping, spinning and smashing their way down a series of standalone, linear levels. When Naughty Dog turned its attention to the PlayStation® 2 there was initially scepticism that a similar game would work on the console due to the harder edged, adult tone with which Sony Computer Entertainment Europe (SCEE) had launched its new console. However, when all the action that characterised a *Crash Bandicoot* title was transposed to

SCEE's brave new world, and with a good measure of technical aplomb, the doubters were silenced.

Appearing early in the life of the PlayStation® 2, the vibrant graphics of *Jak and Daxter* were a great advert for the console's capabilities. But one of the game's most significant technical achievements was that it did away with the notion of disparate, individual levels, by incorporating all of the game's objectives within a single, continuous world. There were no load times. While that might sound underwhelming today, at the time it was a minor revolution. Instead of breaking down the game's tasks into roped-off levels, players could see uninterrupted vistas, spying glimpses of future goals by simply staring over the distant horizons. The game's other major accomplishment from a technical point of view, was the in-game camera, which tracked Jak as he tumbled and leapt through increasingly elaborate areas with barely a glitch or a hiccup.

Naughty Dog's technical proficiency certainly impressed reviewers, but it was less important to the people who played it for fun: more important was the game's rich sense of humour and cast of eccentric characters. First and foremost of these were, of course, the game's eponymous heroes: Jak, the strong and silent type; and Daxter, his garrulous sidekick. Daxter actually starts out as a similar pointy-eared humanoid to Jak, but falls into a pool of a mysterious liquid called Dark Eco only minutes into the opening cut-scene, to be transformed into a short-haired orange rodent. The pair's quest to restore him to

his former state sees them venturing out of their home in Sandover Village with the assistance of the rather ancient sage Samos, and his hot young daughter, Keira.

It sees them venture across the game world to encounter a huge variety of environments and different types of task, from helping out villagers with their fishing at the start of the game, to speeding through canyons on hover bikes and fighting ancient giant robots at the end. It includes every level that you'd expect to see in a platform game, and a little bit more for good measure. Volcanic craters, snowy mountains, forbidden jungles and ancient temples had been seen before of course, but the design skill with which the game gradually reveals these areas, teasing the player with hints of things to come, was wholly original.

Similarly, the game borrows its mechanics and structure from the platform games that preceded it, but it also borrows from other genres and ties it all together with an innovative panache. Jak can spin, punch and jump, just like his predecessors, but he can also sneak and crawl. While he can die, he never runs out of lives – which is handy when going head to head with the game's reptilian baddies, the Lurkers, or up against one of the game's three bosses. Also useful are the various different types of Eco scattered around: Green to heal, Blue for speed, Red for more power, and Yellow to shoot fireballs (and Dark, as Daxter can testify, to be avoided). And where would any platforming game be without the requisite variety of pick-ups? In Jak and Daxter's case, these boil down to Power Cells, which are essential to the pair's progress; Precursor Orbs, which can be used for currency to obtain Power Cells; and Scout Flies which are hidden in each area and also unlock a bonus Power Cell.

In fact, if you look at the individual ingredients, Jak and Daxter actually contains very little that hadn't been seen before in one game or another. But the magpie eye with which the developer ransacked other games and genres for features, and the way in which they were combined resulted in something totally novel. By polishing them to within an inch of their lives, they produced something that still stands out today.

Play it now!

Jak and Daxter inspired several sequels and spin-offs. *Jak II™: Renegade* and *Jak 3™* took the pure platforming of the original, but increased the emphasis on projectile combat, which altered the balance of the game. There's also been a vehicle combat game, *Jak™ X*, and a handheld game on PSP™ (PlayStation® Portable) starring, and named after Jak's sidekick Daxter. While these are all good games, the original and best game in the series is still *The Precursor Legacy*, which is available as part of the Platinum range.

Jet Set Radio Future

Publisher: Sega/Atari
Developer: Sega, Smilebit
Platform: Xbox
Released: 2002

that players join a rollerblading gang, jumping, grinding, tricking and tagging their way across a cel-shaded, futuristic Tokyo, competing with rival gangs for territory and taking on the cops to stick it to the Man – embodied in the game by the sinister mega corporation, Rokkaku Group.

When *Jet Set Radio* arrived on Sega's ill-fated Dreamcast, it was staggeringly, thrillingly new. It wilfully ignored the trend towards photorealism that every other 3D game had pursued since the launch of the PlayStation® to introduce a new visual style called 'cel-shading'. This technique, in which 3D graphics are made to look like hand drawn animation, is now commonplace across all genres, seen more recently in games as diverse as *The Legend of Zelda: The Wind Waker*, and *Ultimate Spider-Man*. Back then it had never been seen before, and was just one example of the way the game defied easy pigeonholing, along with a design that featured a wholly novel combination of extreme rollerblading, exploration, evasion and graffiti. Each level consisted of a busy urban space, with a series of graffiti tags for players to spray over before the cops arrived, and each one was gleaming and vibrant.

Random sample of lyrics featured on the *Jet Set Radio Future* Soundtrack: 'Yes, I'm cooking for my son and his wife/It's his thirtieth birthday/Pour berries into my bowl/Add milk of two months ago/It's mouldy… Mom, isn't it?' It's as good an example as any of the game's slightly baffling, totally kooky, determinedly underground, boldly primary-coloured sense of style. But DJ Professor K's 'out-of-sight sounds' are just the tip of an iceberg of cool. *Jet Set Radio* picks up where the original Dreamcast title left off. Which is to say

Jet Set Radio Future maintained and refined the original game's overwhelming sense of audio-visual sophistication. The energetic sci-fi feel of the cel-shaded graphics were rounded out with a soundtrack rich in subculture chic. It featured artists like Hideki Naganuma (who provided tracks like *Fly Like A Butterfly*, *The Concept of Love*, *Shape Da Future*), the Latch Brothers (*Koto Stomp*), Cibo Matto (the aforementioned *Birthday Cake*), and even a few tracks by cult videogame specialist Richard Jacques. Each new gang was given its

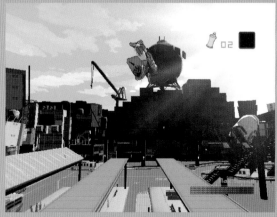

GAME ON

own audio motif and non-stop dance moves, which ranged from a laid-back visual drawl to a high intensity militaristic stomp. And there were the awesomely anime cops: effete bad guys wearing raincoats, or moustachioed, sunglass-wearing spiky-haired dudes, followed by funky-uniformed squads of chanting troopers, or accompanied by helicopters firing menacingly styled homing missiles.

Taking control of 'a group of young kids who've been tearin' up the streets', players navigate through a range of districts, from Shibuya-cho, to Rokkaku-dai Heights, with intricate spaces such as underground sewers to explore in between. One of the principal differences with the original *Jet Set Radio* is that the later version removed the prohibitive countdown timers that limited the extent to which players could investigate their surroundings. One upshot of this was the elaborate extension of environments into dizzying vertical cityscapes – grinding and tricking off advertising hoardings and rails to reach ever-greater heights is one of the game's principal pleasures, and provides some stunning views when you reach the top.

The other major difference is that the tagging system was simplified. Whereas the original Dreamcast game required players to lay down tags by performing complicated button combos, the Xbox sequel featured a streamlined system, requiring just one button press. Again, it changed the emphasis of the game towards more elaborate environments, but it didn't change the fundamentals: lay down a certain number of tags before the inevitable and indomitable wave of cops arrives to complicate matters. As in the original game, new playable characters could be unlocked by recruiting new gang members – usually by beating them in a race. Hot Goth chick Cube, Ulala-alike Gum, bug-eyed Beat, and the boom-box wielding Combo were just some of game's playable gang members, each of whom had different attributes to make them more suited to particular levels or missions.

The game was rounded out by various extra objectives that were to be found in each level, and a series of modes accessible after the game was completed. It also featured a multiplayer mode in which players could tag and grind in competition with each other, and a tag editor which allowed

you to create your own graffiti with which to personalise future Tokyo.

Both versions of *Jet Set Radio* were feted by critics upon their release – deservedly so, since both games are sublimely sassy and cheerfully irreverent, carving out a new set of rules about game design instead of slavishly following what had gone before. Unfortunately, both versions were available exclusively for consoles that were fated for commercial mediocrity, and so neither game performed very well in stores (indeed *Jet Set Radio Future* sold only just over 30,000 copies in its native Japan). Consequently, the chances of a sequel appearing are slim. Which means you owe it to yourself to pick up a second-hand copy while you still can.

Even the cops look cool in Jet Set Radio

Play it now!

Although it's difficult to get hold of a brand new copy of either *Jet Set Radio* or *Jet Set Radio Future*, it's easy enough to get hold of second-hand copies of either on sites like eBay – although you'll need a Dreamcast if you're going to play the original *Jet Set Radio*. And while *Jet Set Radio Future* is playable on Xbox, it hasn't yet made it on to Microsoft's list of backward compatible games for the Xbox 360.

Jet Set Radio Future © SEGA. All Rights Reserved.

The Legend of Zelda™: Ocarina of Time™

Publisher: Nintendo
Developer: Nintendo
Platform: N64
Released: 1998

'Willst thou get the girl?' went the adverts, 'or play like one?' And sure, the fifth chapter in Nintendo's spectacularly successful *Legend of Zelda* series gave players the time-honoured task of saving a princess. Specifically, it gave players control of a young hero on a quest that would take him, and them, across the legendary Kingdom of Hyrule and beyond in his bid to save the world and get the girl. The boy in question was Link, and the girl Zelda. Link's quest would see him gaze upon the sun setting over Hyrule Field, and upon the inside of a giant fish. It would see him accompanied by his loyal steed Epona, and a fairy guide called Navi. It would see him encounter mystical races of people and travel backwards in time in his attempt to recover a mythical artefact called The Triforce, rent asunder into its constituent parts: Power, Wisdom and Courage.

It would be a voyage of discovery for both player and hero – as it presumably was for its developer too, since it was created at a time when 3D games were still in their infancy. Indeed, while the launch of the N64 made a 3D conversion inevitable, it was less obvious how Nintendo would possibly be able to translate all of the design features that had characterised the first four games in the series – features that were much easier to render in two dimensions than three. And yet the renowned design genius of Shigeru Miyamoto would ensure that all of the hallmarks of the series were distilled and enhanced. There was a lot more to this game than just a hokey plot.

He created a game that contained something of everything: combat, platforming, puzzle-solving, exploration, adventure, role-playing, storytelling, and, above all else, the sense that it took place in a living, breathing world. He created a game that would sell 8.6 million copies, propelling the series as a whole to over 47 million copies sold to date; a game that would receive perfect ratings from reviewers across the board – including the notoriously mean magazines *Famitsu* and *Edge*. He created a game that remains, to this day, one

of, if not the most, fondly remembered videogames ever: *The Legend of Zelda: Ocarina of Time*.

The game ran on a modified version of the *Super Mario 64* engine and was, simply, beautiful. Hyrule Kingdom incorporated a plenitude of revelatory views and panoramic vistas. Bewitching, entrancing and wholly convincing, the world contained waterfalls, rivers, deserts and forests. Link's journey would take him from humble beginnings in Kokiri Forest to the underground caverns of Goron city and the watery realms of King Zora, where he would enter the belly of the giant fish Jabu-Jabu. Each new area was realised with an unprecedented degree of authenticity – so setting fire to a Deku stick allowed Zelda to burn cobwebs out of his way, and as day drifted into night, the sun would set and the moon would pass overhead. Each new area provided another visual epiphany, to the extent that a 'Hyrule Field moment' is now shorthand for any moment of awe-inspiring graphical splendour within a videogame.

But Hyrule displayed itself coquettishly: the gradual blossoming outward from the intimate to the epic was one of the game's defining features. It gave the game an addictive hook by granting players a constant sense of achievement; a constant sense that a new discovery was just ahead of them. Link was prevented from fully exploring his world until accomplishing certain goals or discovering certain items allowed access to another part of the kingdom. Finding the Hookshot, for example, would allow Link to pull himself up to high areas that had hitherto remained tantalisingly out of reach – where there would be another teasing hint of what was yet to come. And as the kingdom got larger, Link's means of traversing it got quicker.

His most memorable means of transport was undoubtedly Epona the horse, with whom many gamers would form an emotional attachment out of all proportion to any ordinary videogame. But *Ocarina of Time* is no ordinary videogame, and Epona was entrancing partly because of the game's sublime sense of control. Both Epona and Zelda handled gracefully, jumping automatically and turning on a sixpence.

THE LEGEND OF ZELDA: OCARINA OF TIME

All actions were context-sensitive: press the action button and Link would perform whatever action was appropriate to his circumstances. In combat the L-targeting system – the original target lock system – made sure that control was as accessible and immediate in three dimensions as it had been in two. Throughout the game Link's fairy friend Navi would highlight anything worthy of further investigation, and an inspired interface allowed players to assign weapons and items to any button.

And what a selection of weapons and items! Acquiring and equipping different tunics or boots granted Link various different abilities to assist his explorations, from breathing underwater to hovering over chasms. Other items granted more extraordinary abilities, like the Lens of Truth, which revealed hidden areas and enemy weaknesses. Link's basic armament of sword and shield would benefit from upgrades found across Hyrule, and his armoury gradually expanded to include long-range weapons such as the slingshot and boomerang. And of course there was the eponymous Ocarina of Time.

Within the game, the Ocarina allows Link to learn various melodies with far-reaching consequences: some melodies turn night to day; some change the weather; and some warp Link to new locations. Discovering these melodies constitute quests in their own right, but more significantly, they provide a pretext for the wonderful audio compositions of Koji Kondo, Nintendo's music specialist, who contributed so much to the game's rich atmosphere. This atmosphere is further enhanced by various diversions and mini-games to create the sense of an autonomous universe beyond the game. Helping villagers catch chickens, taking a fishing trip, planting magic beans, finding Fairy Fountains and collecting rupees all brought the Hyrulian landscape to life.

But all these diversions are peripheral to the main quest, and its central dynamic: skipping between time zones to locate seven sages who will help Link unite the three pieces of The Triforce, wrought asunder by the dark-hearted Ganondorf. Leaping forward in time transports Link to a shockingly dystopian future Hyrule – all the more dreadful for its stark contrast with the vibrant pageantry experienced earlier in the game: Goron City lies empty and Zora's Domain is frozen over. But jumping back and forth between time zones allows Link to make minor changes in one zone that have more extensive consequences in the other – solving puzzles that have a temporal dimension in addition to the traditional spatial one.

The climactic showdown with Ganondorf is, when it comes, a fittingly apocalyptic resolution to a tale that has grown magnificently in the telling: from two dimensions on the SNES to three on the N64; from the limited confines of Kokiri Forest to the unbounded streams of time itself; from dodging Deku Scrubs to fighting Ganondorf

himself; and ultimately from a simply sketched 8-bit action game on the NES, to a masterpiece of truly epic and paradigmatic proportions. There is no finer videogame than *Ocarina of Time*.

Play it now!

It's easy enough to get hold of a second-hand copy of the N64 version of *Ocarina of Time*, but it's also relatively easy to find a copy of *The Legend of Zelda: The Wind Waker* for the GameCube, which is bundled with a version of *Ocarina* that will also play on the GameCube. Indeed *The Wind Waker* might fall slightly short of *Ocarina's* majesty, but it's certainly worth playing in its own right. And for those who find their Zelda fix still isn't sated, there are plenty of other titles in the series worth checking out, from forthcoming Wii title *The Twilight Princess*, to old classics, like *A Link to the Past* – available now for the Game Boy Advance.

The Legend of Zelda™: Ocarina of Time™
© 1998 Nintendo.

Lumines

Publisher: Ubisoft (UK) / Bandai (Japan)
Developer: Q Entertainment
Platform: PSP™
Released: 2004

I t's slightly ironic that what might be one of the most beautiful games in the whole book is also, in static pictures, one of the most uninspiring. But still, when you're locked into the game, vision tunelled, it doesn't matter. When you lock into *Lumines* you don't notice the blocks. It's like you see through the screen, and your mind is full of music and colour.

Like many other puzzle games it involves positioning blocks that fall from the top of the screen, aligning them in such a way as to make them disappear when they hit the bottom. *Lumines*' playfield is wider than it is tall, marking a departure from the traditional *Tetris*-style column, one which suits the PSP™'s 16:9 screen perfectly.

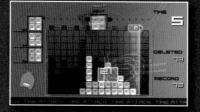

Bear with us while we explain the rules. All of *Lumines* pieces are square and each is made up of four smaller squares. Those smaller squares can be one of two colours, provoking a number (six, in fact) of different types of piece. The pieces must be rotated and positioned as they fall, and your objective is to place them so that their component parts form unicolour blocks at the bottom of the screen. Once *Lumines* notices a player-created unicolour block – say, a rectangle two small squares across and two high – it makes it vanish, and on vanishing any squares above cascade down into the empty space. Those in turn may make

more unicolour blocks, and the pattern continues with a commensurate score reward.

Puzzle games are often confusing to describe, but despite the above paragraph *Lumines*' appeal lies in its simplicity. Once you've grasped the rules there is nothing more to learn, just plans to make and strategies to devise. As is traditional in the genre, progress through the levels brings a marked increase in the speed at which the pieces fall, giving you less time to think and slowly shifting the game from a thoughtful, sedentary experience into one based almost entirely on instinct and reaction. Experienced players begin by planning several moves ahead, and end placing pieces simply to survive long enough to get the next one.

But that isn't the only thing *Lumines* does to mix up the gameplay, and perhaps its smartest twist is yet to be mentioned. A line traces across the playfield every bar, in time with the soundtrack that switches songs every couple of minutes. The line denotes when and where *Lumines* is checking to see if a unicolour block has been formed and though it marks them out as it detects them, it is only when the bar reaches the far right of the screen that the blocks disappear. This brings about two important gameplay effects. First, blocks only ever vanish on the beat, turning the game from a standard puzzle title into something that feels almost like it has elements of rhythm action.

Secondly, it means that your style of play has to alter with the music. Since the speed at which blocks vanish is directly linked to tempo the playfield on slower songs can remain 'unwiped' for a good number of seconds, allowing you to construct intricate cascades of blocks but also threatening you as the screen fills with blocks that will not yet vanish. The fastest songs clear quickly, but creating bigger unicolour blocks is much harder, often produc

NEXT

10:58

SCORE

55239

HI-SCORE

358040

DELETED

329

CHANGE↑
NEXT

SCORE
155545

HI-SCORE
358040

DELETED
1132

LEVEL   58   TIME   27:26

ing a screen which is a cluttered mess of tiny squares. Between the two extremes lies a heap of rich, textured, addictive gameplay, all of which is directly linked to the music.

If the feel of the game didn't make that point clearly enough, the look (the 'skin', in game parlance) switches with each change of song, as does the audio spot effects that come when blocks lock into place and vanish. Some skins provide colour and shape combinations that are easier to get to grips with than others. You will grow to love one look and fear another, and the constant cycling

Play it now!

Lumines is only available for the PSP™, so anyone wanting to block out a few hours in its hypnotic, trance-like environment will need Sony's handheld machine first. However, if you're unsure whether the game will suit you, at the time of writing it's possible to find a number of web games that clone the basic concept, if not the musical aspect so integral to *Lumines*' brilliance.

helps reinforce *Lumines*' mental hypnosis. You're so lost in the game you can barely tell what it looks like. Somehow, you know it looks beautiful.

Its critics have claimed it's too long, and it's true that a single game can last over three hours. It doesn't matter, not just because the PSP™'s stand-by mode means you can drop out and resume in an instant, but because the game puts you in a trance-like state. Those three hours can feel like three minutes and when you close your eyes afterwards you will still see the shapes falling. The mark of a brilliant puzzle game is that it gets inside your head and refuses to get out, even when you switch off. Once you let *Lumines*' rhythm inside you it starts to feel like a heartbeat.

Madden NFL 06

Publisher:	EA Tiburon
Developer:	EA Games
Platform:	Xbox, PlayStation® 2, Xbox 360, GameCube, PSP™
Released:	2005

Madden NFL 06 hits you with the power of a Reggie White sack, and the precision of a Peyton Manning pass: it's got the hardest hits, the strongest stiff-arms, the biggest blitzes and the toughest of tackles. Amazingly lifelike graphics capture everything to do with gridiron, from the physicality of the hits to the perceptive

playbooks. A game can span the course of a single game or entire seasons, and it includes every single NFL player, team, and stadium in existence. It's the latest instalment of a series that has become one of the industry's biggest moneyspinners, and, true to form, it was the top-selling game in North America in the year of its release.

Like the sport it models itself on, it's big, brash and bold, but it also boasts an enormous amount of strategic depth. It's a template that has evolved ever since the first game in the *Madden* series was commissioned for the Apple II, way back in 1984. But it wasn't till *John Madden Football* appeared on Sega's Mega Drive in 1990 that the series hit the big time, paving the way for a blockbusting new instalment every subsequent year. The game's enormous success has helped to establish publisher Electronic Arts as a corporate behemoth and the world's largest independent publisher, with a net revenue of over $3 billion in 2005.

Over the course of the series, new features have accu-

mulated around a framework laid down by that original Mega Drive game which has remained pretty consistent. Pick a team, win the toss, choose your formation, select a play, and put it into practice on the pitch. Once you're out on the pitch, you control your quarterback, runners and receivers on offense, and the player nearest the ball on defense. That much has remained constant over the years, but with each new instalment has come a raft of inspired additions. The mix has been maxed by adding new stadiums, more formations, further playbooks (and eventually play editors to allow players to design their own strategies), a wider range of weather conditions, new player moves, and more and more game stats. One major development was the move from isometric graphics to fully 3D visuals when *John Madden Football 97* arrived on the PlayStation® in 1996, and online competition was introduced thanks to the

network functionality of PlayStation® 2 and Xbox.

With each passing year, *Madden* has relentlessly set the benchmark for American Football videogames, providing its copycat competitors with, first, its passing window system (in which your receivers are highlighted in three windows across the top of the screen), and then the more authentic windowless system. Player drafts have been introduced, multiple season campaigns included, and real-life rules added, such as the ability to adjust your tactics from the line of scrimmage by calling an audible. It's got everything you'd expect from a football game: special teams, two-minute drills, no huddle offenses, sprints, slides, dives, spins, stiff-arms, blitzing, play actions, I-form, singleback, split backs, weak I, goal line, shotgun, classic teams, current teams... As EA's marketing tagline says, 'If it's in the game, it's in the game.'

That includes, of course, the commentary. John Madden's record as an NFL coach is actually hugely impressive: he coached the Oakland Raiders from 1969

for ten years, winning a Super Bowl in 1977 and achieving the highest regular season winning percentage (.759) for a coach in NFL history with over 100 career wins. And yet he's probably better known by a whole generation of people (certainly in Europe) as a character in a videogame. In *Madden 06* he returns (though controversially, not in the Xbox 360 version) with his real-life co-commentator, Al Michaels, to once again provide the voiceover for a game that encapsulates everything about everything to do with the pigskin.

And *Madden 06* has come a long way since even the first PlayStation® 2 title, *Madden 2001*. Quite apart from the huge leap in visual brilliance, yet more new features have been added, such as QB Vision Control, which simulates the quarterback's field of vision (pass to a receiver on the periphery of his vision and it'll be harder to complete). Or such as another innovation, Precision Passing, which grants players even greater control over passing plays by allowing quarterbacks to deliver the ball in front or behind their receiver in anticipation of their running patterns. And the Xbox 360 version? That'll just have the most amazing graphics ever seen in a sports game on a home console, then.

Part of *Madden*'s appeal is undoubtedly that American Football is itself so inordinately suited for videogame conversion, combining turn-based strategy with real-time action to provide intelligence *and* action. But *Madden* isn't the only game to try to faithfully reproduce America's greatest ever sport: it's just the best game to do so. And *Madden 06* is the zenith of the series so far.

Play it now!

Madden NFL 06 is currently available to play for every major current format. While previous versions of the *Madden* franchise are also available on every format except PSP™ and Xbox 360, EA no longer supports the online functionality of these earlier versions, so it's not possible to play them against online opponents.

Mario Kart™ DS

Publisher: Nintendo
Developer: Nintendo
Platform: Nintendo DS
Released: 2005

Super Mario Kart was the original kart game and, thanks to the latest update on Nintendo's DS, it's still the best. The original game took the best known characters from perhaps the best-loved videogame series and took what was then an unusual step: putting them in karts. It gave them some amazing tracks to race around, based on some of the most fondly remembered platform levels, it gave them a simple, but sophisticated handling model, and it depicted them in near 3D thanks to the Super Nintendo's Mode 7 graphical capabilities.

Subsequent games in the series managed the transition to true 3D by ramping up the effects of power-ups, enhancing multiplayer modes, and creating ever more elaborate tracks and courses. The DS version of Mario Kart uses Nintendo's dual screens to offer more feedback to the player, but it also distils the best features of each sequel and includes the most memorable race tracks from the entire series, making it the best game in the series so far, and one of the best racing games ever.

The essence of the game was the simplicity and purity of its handling and it still is. Accelerating, braking and steering are all exceedingly easy to perform, but various tricks and techniques allow experts to squeeze out every last smidgen of speed. Hopping grants players extra manoeuvrability to make sure they stay on the racing line, drifting allows them to maintain their speed, and managing to pull off a mini-turbo boost saves even more seconds. And if you're aiming for the best possible time, you'll need to accelerate at precisely the right moment from the starting line to gain a turbo start and an advantage over the other racers.

Six of the original eight racers return in the DS game, joined by several new additions and one or two unlockable extras, and, as ever, the cloud-riding Lakitu floats overhead to retrieve competitors if they stray too far from the race track.

The original *Mario Kart*'s real masterstroke of genius was that the deceptively simple handling model allowed each character to possess significantly different characteristics – a feature that *Mario Kart DS*, like *Double Dash!!* on the GameCube enhances by allowing players to pick different karts which adjust those characteristics.

Unsurprisingly, Mario and Luigi set the default standard, presenting a balanced mix of acceleration, handling and top speed that's perfect for beginners. Racers like Yoshi and Princess might have the edge on acceleration, while Toad has superior handling, but the choice of experts is still the heavyweights – racing daddies like Wario or Bowser, both bruisers who can buffet others out of their path with ease. Emphatically *not* for beginners, they take ages to hit top speed, but when they get there they're faster than the rest. So just as long as they don't hit anything, they're by far the best.

The other thing to return in *Mario Kart DS* is the choice of universally excellent courses. The highlights of the game's 16 new tracks include some dizzyingly topsy-turvy delights, such as Waluigi Pinball, Tick-Tock Clock and DK Pass, and there's a stunning new variation of Rainbow Road which pushes racers to the limits of their control, punishing any mistake with the

sheer drops at the edge of the track. But brilliantly the game also includes a Retro Grand Prix mode which includes 16 tracks drawn from all of the games in the series so far – so the new tracks rub shoulders with the likes of Choco Island 2 (*Super Mario Kart*), Banshee Boardwalk (*Mario Kart 64*), Sky Garden (*Super Circuit*) and Baby Park (*Double Dash!!*).

Speed boosts, jumps and environmental obstacles such as oil slicks and mud patches continue to make life more difficult for drivers, as do course inhabitants like Thrumps (falling blocks of concrete) and Gophers (who popped out of the ground). But various shortcuts make life easier, even if most of them require the right power-up and/or various degrees of skill to pull off. Indeed the DS includes the most balanced range of power-ups in the series so far: mushrooms provide a burst of speed; bananas get in the way of other

143

LAP 2/3

4th

1
2
3
4
5
6
7
8

LAP 7/3

TIME 0:47:37

LAP 7

8th

GAME ON

racers; green and red shells can be used defensively or offensively; and the dreaded blue shell allows back markers to get their revenge on the race leader. Again, advanced tactics gives experts an edge, since weapons can be thrown or left behind.

In singleplayer modes, player once again compete against the clock or against other racers to unlock new competitions at higher speeds. A new feature is the Missions mode, which consists of a series of short tests of driving skill along the lines of *Gran Turismo*'s licence tests. But the game's real substance is in its multiplayer modes, against other AI racers, or, thanks to the Wi-Fi feature of the DS, in a head-to-head race against another human opponent. Again, the battle mode has been enhanced by the addition of Shine Runners to the usual Balloon Battle.

The utter brilliance of the original *Mario Kart* inspired several sequels on later consoles. The N64 version introduced 3D courses and a wider range of power-ups to shift the emphasis from the purity of the racing model to the ploys of the various racers. It also extended the multiplayer modes to include up to four players. The balance returned to the racing itself with the magnificent GBA version. Like the original, picking coins up around the course increases the speed of the karts, and power slides were given an extra edge, as they had been on the N64. On the GameCube, *Double Dash!!* returned, once again, to the party game vibe of the N64 version.

Mario Kart DS takes each of these new additions and refines them and hones them. It takes the unsurpassed emphasis on handling of the original game, throws in the extended roster of power-ups from *Mario Kart 64*, with a dash of the unrivalled course design from *Super Circuit* and a smidgeon of multiplayer mayhem inspired by *Double Dash!!* While most other kart games are lazy attempts to milk more money from videogame characters that are on their last legs, the original, and still the best kart game continues to hop, drift and turbo its way from strength to strength.

Play it now!

Mario Kart DS is still available to play on the Nintendo DS. *Double Dash!!* is also still available on the GameCube, but for previous games in the series, you'll need to search second-hand stores for previously owned consoles and cartridges. There's also the possibility that earlier *Mario Kart*s will be available to play on Nintendo's new Wii. It's certainly worth trying them all.

Mario Kart™ *DS* © 2005 Nintendo.

Metal Gear Solid

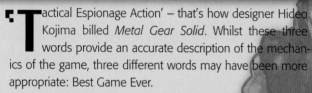

Publisher: Konami Europe
Developer: Konami Computer Entertainment Japan, Inc.
Platform: PlayStation®, PC
Released: 1998

'Tactical Espionage Action' – that's how designer Hideo Kojima billed *Metal Gear Solid*. Whilst these three words provide an accurate description of the mechanics of the game, three different words may have been more appropriate: Best Game Ever.

And it was, at the time. *Metal Gear Solid* was the first game to really demonstrate the power of the PlayStation®. Stunning 3D visuals, Hollywood-style cut-scenes coupled with some of gaming's most memorable set pieces – this was an event release unlike anything seen before.

Set in what was then the near future – but is now actually the recent past – *Metal Gear Solid* introduced Solid Snake, an elite super-spy charged with infiltrating a nuclear weapons disposal facility which has been taken over by terrorists. Seizing control of Metal Gear – a nuclear weapon capable of destroying any target on earth – these terrorists demand the body of

their fallen leader, Big Boss. What at first seems like a standard assignment becomes a battle against insurmountable odds, where no one can be trusted and nothing is as it seems.

Solid Snake actually featured in two previous games on the MSX2 and Nintendo Entertainment System, but his appearance on PlayStation® was the first time he'd made such an impact. This is mainly due to the visuals – it's fair to say nothing of this quality and ambition had ever been seen outside of movies before. But *Metal Gear Solid* was so much more than sophisticated eye candy – its self-referential humour and gaming innovations redefined the way we appreciate the medium.

Metal Gear Solid frequently surprised players by using real-world mechanics within its virtual environment. The first instance of this is when Snake's commander, Colonel Campbell, asks Snake to input a radio frequency which can be found on the back of the game's packaging. Next, one of the game's boss characters covertly reads the player's PlayStation® memory card – and if selected Konami game saves are present, he'll comment on them. He also asks the player to place the DualShock controller on the floor, making it move as if to illustrate his psychic powers. And this particular character can only be defeated by physically altering something on the console itself in order to stop him reading the player's inputs. We'll not spoil it for you – it's a moment of revelation which should be enjoyed by all.

GAME ON

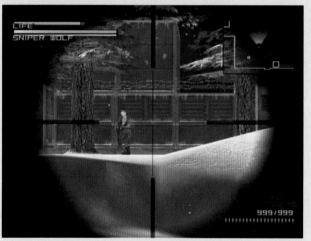

But it wasn't just a few cheap gimmicks which made *Metal Gear Solid* one of PlayStation®'s most celebrated releases. By relying as much on stealth as it did action, it was a new way of playing. With the odds stacked against Snake from the off, it was not uncommon to remain hidden in one location for upwards of five minutes as patrolling guards' patterns were memorised. The huge red exclamation mark and accompanying screech which marked the player being spotted would rank as one of the most terrifying moments in gaming.

And whilst the plot was convoluted and the in-game conversations often intrusive, it all hung together, illustrating a degree of maturity rarely seen in interactive scriptwriting. A cursed bunch of adversaries and a real sense of foreboding made this an incredibly dark adventure, where even the death of a bad guy was difficult to celebrate. Kojima wrote the game as a commentary on love, death and the sense of self – as

well as a stance against nuclear weapons. Few games can boast such morality.

The popularity of the *Metal Gear* series and of *MGS* in particular influenced the design of many subsequent video-games. The stealth mechanic proved that games-players didn't just want to hold down X to shoot; sometimes, hiding in the shadows was equally satisfying. As such, it's reasonable to assume that *Splinter Cell*'s Sam Fisher wouldn't have seen the light of day had Solid Snake not spent so much time in the dark.

Metal Gear Solid was followed three years later by a hugely anticipated sequel, subtitled *Sons of Liberty* for PlayStation® 2. Again, Kojima proved canny, releasing a game completely different to the one the press and public were expecting. Indeed, as the first act closed, *Metal Gear Solid 2* seemed to be at odds with its title – a move which proved as controversial as it was clever. Whilst the game's plot was at best a rambling mess (illustrated by the fact that the post 9-11 removal of a cut-scene showing Manhattan being destroyed probably

wasn't noticed by players so baffled by the bluffs and double bluffs), the game itself was another master class in technology and design.

An enhanced version of *Metal Gear Solid* was ported to the GameCube in 2004. Subtitled *The Twin Snakes*, it was *Metal Gear Solid* with *Sons of Liberty*'s graphics and a few gameplay tweaks. Developed by Nintendo second-party team Silicon Knights in collaboration with Japanese film director Ryuhei Kitamura, it marks the definitive version of the game. *Metal Gear Solid 3: Snake Eater* appeared on PlayStation® 2 in 2005, set prior to the original *Metal Gear Solid*. However, its controversial removal of the game's trademark radar frustrated some of the series' die-hard fans.

Metal Gear's extensive history has offered Konami scope to produce many spin-offs and companion titles. A Game Boy Color release in 2000 crammed virtually the entire *Metal Gear Solid* plot into a top-down adventure, set outside the main series chronology. *Metal Gear Ac!d* (2005) and *Metal Gear Ac!d 2* (2006) on PSP™ took Solid Snake in an entirely new turn-based direction, as players used strategic cards to issue instructions. Additionally, Virtual Missions and re-releases with additional levels have cropped up on both PlayStation® and Xbox.

Though not a Sony exclusive, *Metal Gear Solid* is perhaps the format's most celebrated franchise, selling the hardware almost as much as software. Kojima has announced plans to be less hands-on with the forthcoming sequel, co-directing *Metal Gear Solid: Guns of the Patriots* rather than directing, indicating he wants to conclude the series with a bang, wrapping up the loose ends and answering those questions left unanswered. Of course, it's Kojima's prerogative to conclude the series whenever he wishes. Games players the world over, however, would prefer that he never did.

Play it now!

With GameCube compatible with the Nintendo Wii, *The Twin Snakes* offers the most complete way of enjoying the original *Metal Gear Solid*. *Metal Gear Solid: Guns of the Patriots* (above) is scheduled for release on PlayStation® 3 in early 2007, promising fully destructible terrain for the first time in the series. Whilst this new mechanic sounds appealing, *MGS3*'s tinkering arguably spoilt the experience. One hopes Kojima will have learnt his lesson.

OutRun

Publisher: Sega
Developer: Sega-AM2
Platform: Arcade, various
Released: 1986

Imagine: sitting back in your classic sports convertible, sun glinting off the bonnet, sea breeze ruffling through your hair, trophy bottle-blonde girlfriend by your side as you get ready to whack up the stereo, open up the throttle and weave in and out of the beachfront traffic because … well, just because you can. Some games create a photorealistic simulation of the world in all its oily, nitty-gritty glory. *OutRun* creates a sense of pure, unadulterated, escapist bliss. It proved to be a startlingly revelatory experience back in 1986. Its hydraulic cabinet, glorious soundtrack, and the blue skies, golden sands, and gleaming red car supplied an unprecedented, exhilarating rush. And it's still one of the best racing games released for the arcade.

The game was created by one of Sega's legendary designers, Yu Suzuki, whose CV includes several other seminal games, including *Hang-On*, *Virtua Fighter*, *Space Harrier*, and *Shenmue*. Indeed, eagle-eyed observers would notice that holding the Start button while approaching a checkpoint would flash up the following message: 'Program by Yu Suzuki 1986 Sep.'. But you didn't need eagle eyes to notice the game's most obvious attraction: its cabinet. It came in four different shapes, each of them a gleaming, enticing advertisement for the vivid worlds within. Two upright versions featured a steering wheel, gear shift, gas and brake pedals but the real daddy was the sit-down version that used hydraulics to shake and shudder in synch with the action onscreen. With this sort of technology restricted to just a handful of titles (such as Sega's own *After Burner II*), it was a standout sight wherever it was located.

After sticking your money in the machine, the next thing that competed for your rapt attention was an unbelievable soundtrack, composed by Hiroshi Miyauchi – Sega's arcade soundtrack specialist. Making use of the machine's Yamaha YM2151 soundchip, it excelled in terms of fidelity and hummability: even today, tracks like *Magical Sound Shower* inspire fervent memories. There were actually only three tunes (the other two were *Passing Breeze* and *Splash Wave*), but players could choose these from the in-game car stereo at the start of the game, and a fourth tune, *Last Wave*, played if you achieved a high score.

And finally, there were the graphics: technically innovative and boldly stylish, they were also breathtaking and revelatory. Although not properly 3D, the game made use of inventive new sprite-scaling techniques to create the impression of three dimensions. It was the second Sega title after *Space Harrier* to feature 'Super-Scaler' technology; which allowed the game to employ a 'chase cam' view, in contrast to the overhead views that characterised most other racing games.

Consequently, the rolling hills, sweeping curves, and rapid transitions between night and day provided some stunning visual set-pieces. Crashes were equally spectacular: take a bend badly and the car would skid round 360 degrees; hit another vehicle and the car would roll and flip sensationally (an aspect that would be revisited in modern titles such as the *BurnOut* series).

In terms of handling, the main challenge was avoiding other traffic while taking the racing line, and using the gears to get the best performance: using the low gear to build up speed or hold the road while taking bends; and shifting into high gear to hit top speed on open straights. Another knack was mastering the art of using the low gear to reduce speed, instead of braking suddenly and losing momentum. Losing momentum was to be avoided at all costs if you wanted to hit every checkpoint and impress onlookers by haring down the final stretch of the game's choose-your-own route.

computer version). Insert your audio cassette, turn up the volume and press play to experience the full sound effects and make this a thrilling audio/visual sensation, while you play *OUT RUN!*

Of course, technology has moved on now, and home consoles are more than capable of reproducing *OutRun*'s soundtrack without the use of innovative 'Hi-Fi' peripheral technology. *OutRun*, too, has moved on, thanks to a couple of recent sequels which update the game's visual flamboyance for the modern era, throwing in a gleefully satisfying powerslide mechanic for good measure. But the original *OutRun* is still one of the defining moments in videogame history – a *Passing Breeze* with the emotional impact of a hurricane.

OutRun's appeal was massive. It was converted for almost every home system – with mixed results. Unlike modern day platform conversions, early '80s ports were usually farmed out to independent developers who were given little support, or even original code. Consequently, many home versions of *OutRun* were created from scratch, by designers who would play the game in arcades and copy down the original graphics by hand (though this didn't stop publishers from using original arcade screens on the packaging of home conversions...). Thus, they varied enormously in quality, from the pretty poor Spectrum and Amiga versions to the near perfect Saturn or PC Engine ports. One thing that was consistent in quality though, was the soundtrack, which accompanied several console versions on audiocassette. From the manual:

'To use the audio tape, first load your program following the loading instructions for your computer. Toggle off the music (if music is included on your

Play it now!

Apart from second-hand copies and emulated versions of dubious legality, it's possible to play versions of the original *OutRun* on several current home consoles. In the Xbox RPG *Shenmue II*, for example, it's possible to enter an arcade which features a fully working *OutRun* cabinet, or if you have a Japanese PlayStation® 2 it's possible to play a graphically updated version of the game thanks to the Sega AGES series. But the best place to play the original game is as an unlockable within *OutRun 2*, a stunning game in its own right which is available on Xbox (and which has its own, equally awesome sequel, *OutRun 2006: Coast 2 Coast*, available on Xbox, PlayStation® 2, PSP™ and PC).

Publisher: Midway
Developer: Namco
Platform: Arcade
Released: 1980

'It's stupid to say that computer games have bad influence on children. If *Pac-Man* had influenced children born in the 80s, today we'd have lots of kids running around in dark rooms eating pills, while listening to monotonous and dull electronic music…'

So, reportedly, joked Nintendo Inc's Kristian Wilson in 1989. The quote remains popular today, continuing to adorn the clothing of videogames fans the world over illustrating not just the quality of the gag but the continued affinity for the seminal *Pac-Man* character, who burst onto the scene in 1980.

Designer Toru Iwatani's inspiration for the spherical yellow hero came from a pizza with a slice missing. After considering the shape of his partially consumed snack, Iwatani set about designing a videogame which would incorporate the outline, in a game based around eating. Given that 'Puck-Man' – a loose translation of the original Japanese name was changed by publisher Midway on the premise that the first letter could be easily defaced to an 'F', be thankful Iwatani wasn't eating one sausage and a couple of eggs when his original idea struck. Imagine the outcry.

Though the concept of a game featuring a hero with no arms or legs was unusual, in practice it proved sound but, surprisingly, it took time for the game to become popular in Japan, which was too busy embracing space combat games of the *Space Invaders* ilk. America, however, embraced the idea of a videogame which wasn't overtly focused on shooting – and the game's popularity soon spread throughout the world. It's not waned signifi-

CHARACTER	/	NICKNAME
- SHADOW		"BLINKY"
- SPEEDY		"PINKY"
- BASHFUL		"INKY"
- POKEY		"CLYDE"

- 10 PTS
- 50 PTS

ghosts – Inky, Blinky, Pinky and Clyde. If a ghost touches Pac-Man, he loses a life. Repeat until fade.

A brief respite is offered in the form of four 'power pellets' on each level. These offer Pac-Man a short period of time in which to turn the tables and chase the ghosts. If he touches one whilst the power pellet is active, he bags some points and sends them scampering back to their base. After a short period, they re-emerge and begin the hunt again. Once a maze is cleared, it's onto another. As with most games of the period, it's all about the high scores.

Whilst the vast majority of *Pac-Man* players were casual gamers simply happy to enjoy a few minutes' entertainment from their quarter, a dedicated band of hardcore players began to dissect the game's intricacies. It was discovered that the ghosts were far more than just differently-coloured sprites – instead programmed with a slightly different chase algorithms which could be exploited by those in the know. These aficionados also learnt that Pac-Man turned corners slightly quicker than his pursuers, and that he travelled 20 per cent faster through corridors cleared of dots. Additionally, they realised that the ghosts would avoid certain tunnels or get confused if Pac-Man remained in one position. The latter strategy was employed when players took toilet breaks whilst going for the 'perfect game'.

Whilst the game should continue infinitely provided the player retains his lives, a technical glitch in the original arcade board means that *Pac-Man* has only 255 playable mazes. For 18 years, achieving the perfect score of 3,333,360 – all dots, power pellets and ghosts without losing one life – was videogaming's Holy Grail. It was finally achieved in 1999 by Billy Mitchell, Fort Lauderdale, who played for six hours

Pac-Man's popularity almost brought Atari to its knees in the early eighties. The publisher snapped up the first home console rights for its Atari 2600 console, but shipped a terrible version riddled with graphical glitches, and bereft of the original's charm. So what should have been a sure-fire hit turned out to be a crippling blow. It didn't help that the publisher was so confident in the success of this port that it is rumoured to have manufactured 12 million cartridges despite the fact there were only 10 million consoles in the market at the time.

Atari's conversion aside, *Pac-Man* has been a universal success, spawning countless sequels and spin-offs and even making guest appearances in other games. His popularity continues to this day: *Pac-Man World 3* – a 3D action adventure – was released for PlayStation® 2, Xbox, PSP™, Game Cube and PC as recently as Christmas 2005, with the hero's voice heard for the first time ever in a game.

Whilst tastes progress and games become increasingly complicated, something with the simplicity of *Pac-Man* would struggle to make an impact these days. But in 1980, make an impact he did – and *Pac-Man* has earned a permanent place in our hearts. But, twenty-six years on, he remains as fresh as ever. One dreads to think what Lara Croft will look like after a quarter of a century.

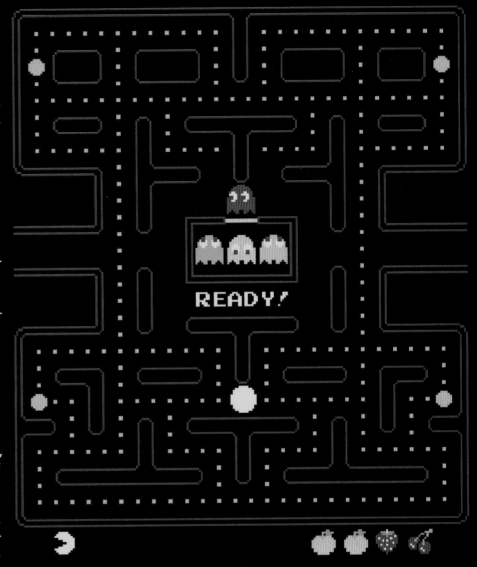

Play it now!

Pac-Man is available for most mobile phones – but perhaps the best way to play it these days is as an unlockable bonus in *Ridge Racer 6* on Xbox 360. It doesn't really benefit from high-definition televisions, though.

Pac-Man™ © NAMCO BANDAI Games Inc.

Pokémon™ Ruby/ Sapphire

Hi! Sorry to keep you waiting!

This is what we call a "POKéMON."

Are you a boy?
Or are you a girl?

Publisher: Nintendo
Developer: Game Freak
Platform: GameBoy Advance
Released: 2003

P okémon is a marketing phenomenon. Its original re-lease, in 1996, spawned a merchandising juggernaut that's still going strong today. Appearing on the cover of *Time* magazine in 1999, the series has straddled trading cards, toys, books, comics, (allegedly epilepsy-inducing-) cartoons, magazines, movies, and even papal proclamations. It inspired one eight-year-old boy to try to trade his sister for a Vaporeon, and prompted a law suit by Israeli psychic and friend-to-Michael-Jackson Uri Geller. It's even inspired its own videogame spin-offs, such as *Pokémon Snap*, *Stadium* and *Pinball*. But this tidal wave of associated activities obscures the nature of the games that lie at the heart of the phenomenon. Because at the heart of that phenomenon is a series of videogames. Very good videogames.

It's a series that has sold over 143 million videogames in its lifetime, making it one of the most successful videogame series ever, second only to *Mario*. It was created in 1996 by Satoshi Tajiri, inspired by his childhood hobby of insect collecting, and it takes its western name from an abbreviation of its Japanese name, *Pocket Monster*. And while its marketing tagline, 'gotta catch 'em all' is absolutely appropriate, it doesn't quite capture the dizzying vistas of complexity that await players – particularly those who approach this game expecting a kiddy's toy.

Still, the central premise behind the design of the game and the success of its merchandising *is* the collection of every single possible Pokémon. Originally num-bering 151, the full roster of Pokémon now reaches a tally of 395, and the game is designed to appeal to the obsessive compulsive in all of us, with no single game in the core series featuring all 395. Consequently, players (known as trainers in the game) need to trade with other trainers to get hold of the rarer species, or they must take sufficient care of their Pokémon to cause them to evolve into new species. The Pokémon themselves are largely inspired by real life fauna, like Beautifly (butter-fly), Zigzagoon (raccoon) or Tentacruel (jellyfish). Others are of more exotic origin, such as Kadabra (the cause of the aforementioned – unsuccessful – law suit), or Xatu (possibly inspired by an Aztec deity), or Jirachi (some sort of good-luck sprite). And some are destined for more fame than others, as Pikachu and Jigglypuff can attest.

YOUR NAME?
▶ TAURUS_

A B C D E F .
G H I J K L ;
M N O P Q R S
T U V W X Y Z

lower
SELECT ▶

BACK
Ⓑ BUTTON

O K
START ▶

Ⓐ BUTTON TO SELECT

The basic framework of the game bearing their name was established in the original Game Boy games, *Pokémon Red* and *Pokémon Blue*, and at its heart is the classic RPG structure: players travel between villages that are separated by wild areas; acquiring new items or skills allows them to reach new parts of the map; and as the map gets larger it becomes easier to circumnavigate thanks to quicker modes of transport. The object of the game was to search wilderness areas for Pokémon and catch them using Pokéballs, before training them to assemble a fighting team. Over the course of the game, trainers would be spurred on by a series of ongoing encounters with their rival – an NPC who would show up at key points in the game – and would ultimately take on the game's eight gym leaders and the 'Elite Four' Pokémon trainers.

But the game continued long after this objective was achieved thanks to a multiplayer dimension that was central to the game design: there were 11 Pokémon exclusive to each different colour version of the game, and three starting

Pokémon that weren't available anywhere else in the game (Bulbasaur, Charmander and Squirtle in the original title). Thus the game design required players to link up with their friends in order to trade Pokémon and show off their prowess as traders – a social aspect that was a masterstroke of design.

Treecko Grovyle Sceptile Torchic Combusken Blaziken Mudkip Marshtomp Swampert Poochyena Mightyena Zigzagoon Linoone Wurmple Silco

eautifly Cascoon Dustox Lotad Lombre Ludicolo Seedot Nuzleaf Shiftry Nincada Ninjask Shedinja Taillow Swellow Shro

Breloom Spinda Wingull Pelipper Surskit Masquerain Wailmer Wailord Skitty Delcatty Kecleon Baltoy Claydol Nosepass To

Sableye Barboach Whiscash Luvdisc Corphish Crawdaunt Feebas Milotic Carvanha Sharpedo Trapinch Vibrava Flygon Makuhita Ha

Electrike Manectric Numel Camerupt Spheal Sealeo Walrein Cacnea Cacturne Snorunt Glalie Lunatone Solrock Azurill Sp

Grumpig Plusle Minun Mawile Meditite Medicham Swablu Altaria Wynaut Duskull Dusclops Roselia Slakoth Vigoroth Sla

Gulpin Swalot Tropius Whismur Loudred Exploud Clamperl Huntail Gorebyss Absol Shuppet Banette Seviper Zangoose Relic

Aron Lairon Aggron Castform Volbeat Illumise Lileep Cradily Anorith Armaldo Ralts Kirlia Gardevoir Bagon She

alamence Beldum Metang Metagross Regirock Regice Registeel Kyogre Groudon Rayquaza Latias Latios Jirachi Deoxys Chi

GAME ON

PROF. BIRCH spends days in his LAB studying, then he'll suddenly go out in

The other masterstroke was the combat system that lay at the heart of the game: a paper-scissors-stone rule system that determines the results of any encounter between Pokémon. Indeed although Pokémon can never die, the substance of the game in both single and multiplayer is the combat between Pokémon. To the untrained eye the game's central mystery might be how it managed to capture the hearts and minds of a generation of kids characterised by super-short attention spans: the majority of the game is spent indulging in turn-based con-

tests displayed with minimal graphical flourish.

But actually, kids aren't stupid. One reason that successive generations of trainers have remained transfixed by the game is that a simple set of underlying rules are capable of generating a satisfyingly sophisticated strategic challenge. In addition to their special abilities and customisable attacks, each Pokémon belongs to one of 17 different types. Just as paper trumps stone in the playground game, but is itself trumped by scissors, so different Pokémon will trump others and, in turn, be trumped by others: Pokémon attacks are super effective, effective, not very effective, or have no effect. Layered on top of this system are the individual attacks of the various Pokémon, some of which have special effects like Poison, or Sleep. It's a devastatingly simple system and ultimately, it's the powerhouse behind the marketing behemoth that surrounds the game.

In my BAG!
There's a POKé BALL!

**CHICK POKéMON
TORCHIC**

PROF. BIRCH is in trouble!
Release a POKéMON and rescue him!

Every game in the series since has built upon these basics to create an increasingly honed challenge which reached its highest point (so far) on the Game Boy Advance in the shape of *Pokémon Ruby* and *Pokémon Sapphire*. Unsurprisingly the game is graphically superior to its forebears, but it's also more satisfyingly complex – keeping the RPG outline intact but enhanced and extending the Pokédex to 200 (the starting Pokémon are Treecko, Torchic and Mudkip). The game begins in Littleroot Town and players take on the role of either Brendan (male) or May (um … female). New features include Pokémon Contests, which allow trainers to show off their Pokémon without risking them in combat; new abilities inherent to certain Pokémon; two on two battles; and Poké-blocks (a form of Pokémon multivitamin, created by planting berries and combining them in a minigame).

But like the other games in the series, *Pokémon Ruby* and *Sapphire* allow players to dictate their own terms. Trainers can choose to focus on creating a specialised squad of Poké-fighters by concentrating their training on just their favourite few, or they can assemble an entire army of less intensively reared Pokémon; they can choose to spend their time taking on other trainers, or simply collecting as many Pokémon as they can. *Pokémon* is a phenomenon that's large enough to contain multitudes.

Choose a POKéMON.

I'd like you to have the POKéMON you used earlier.▼

We sell a variety of goods including POKé BALLS for catching POKéMON.▼

We've restored your POKéMON to full health.

My POKéMON is staggeringly tired... I should have brought a POTION...

You may trade your POKéMON here with a friend.▼

TRIFORCE♂   L:7
15/25

Wow! That's great! TAURUS, you're pretty good!

Play it now!

Pokémon Ruby and Sapphire are both available for the Game Boy Advance. Also available are Pokémon Fire Red and Leaf Green, remakes of the original Game Boy Pokémon games, updated for compatibility with Ruby and Sapphire. Nintendo's DS has yet to receive a proper Pokémon title, but is home to two Pokémon puzzlers, Pokémon Link and Pokémon Dash.

Pong

Publisher: Atari
Developer: Atari
Platform: Arcade
Released: 1972

I t's a multi-billion-dollar industry, recognised as one of the most creative, powerful and valuable in the world. Videogames touch billions of players across a variety of formats, from PlayStation™ to mobile phones, interactive TV and PDAs. It's controversial, educational, enabling, demeaning, infantile and mature, depending on your social and political perspective. And it can be pretty much attributed to one man that few will have heard of.

Born in 1922 in south west Germany, Ralf Baer certainly wouldn't fit in with today's typical games designer. A radio service technician originally, he fought in World War I before moving into television, graduating at the American Television Institute of Technology in 1949. Whilst the concept of playing games cannot be considered his, he filed the first ever patent for playing them on a TV set. His ideas would eventually result in the production of the Magnavox Odyssey, a primitive home console released in 1972.

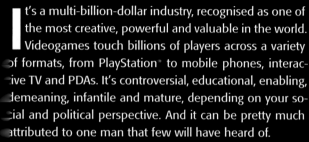

One of the earliest games playable on the Odyssey during its development was *Ping-Pong*, which was up and running on the prototype on 11 November 1967. As the system was being demonstrated at technology fairs around America, a young Nolan Bushnell stumbled across this primitive *Ping-Pong* game. Shortly after, he formed a company called Atari – and its first project commercial release was an arcade game called *Pong*.

The game was actually the result of a challenge Bushnell made of programmer Al Acorn. Al was employed to code games; the only slight problem was his inexperience in this field. Bushnell asked him to create a simple *Ping-Pong* game in order to familiarise himself with the fundamentals of coding before moving on to more complicated designs. However, the result proved so playable they decided to trial a few arcade cabinets.

Pong was unlike anything the public had seen before. Two early field tests in bars drew huge crowds; excess coins prompted one machine to malfunction. Its simplicity proved sensational. It was easy enough for anyone to enjoy, and particularly those who were inebriated.

Indeed, in a medium these days populated by huge manuals and even larger tips books, the instructions for the world's first massively popular arcade video game are laughably simple: 'Avoid missing ball for high score'. History shows that the instruction 'Insert Coin' proved equally seductive.

However, its similarity to *Ping-Pong* wasn't enjoyed by all. Magnavox and Atari subsequently battled in court, with Bushnell's company eventually paying a one-off licensing fee. This was a shrewd move – *Pong* established the arcade industry, enjoying huge success on its full commercial rollout.

But this wasn't enough for Bushnell, who realised he was on to something special. He believed Atari could kickstart the home market, too, despite the fact that the Magnavox Odyssey had failed so dismally (it was actually discontinued in 1974, after less than two years on the market). Nevertheless, Atari pushed ahead with a home prototype, and in 1975 it was the must-have Christmas present, prompting queues around the block whenever stores replenished their supplies.

Home Pong cost $100 on its release – hugely expensive for the time. But nonetheless it convinced the public that home gaming was a hobby worth investing in and a hugely enjoyable pastime. Sure, had Baer and Bushnell not invented *Ping-Pong* and *Pong*, someone else would. Baer's technical and design skills with Bushnell's entrepreneurial nous proved a formidable combination. Those teenagers weaned on *Home Pong* now have families, most of which have a home console under their television.

Pong was also to prove the first victim of a typical videogame malaise as its popularity convinced Atari and countless other companies that the public would sustain an increasing number of variations. Whilst there's little doubt of the affection *Pong* holds, this couldn't support the number of official and unofficial games which have appeared over the years – including an ill-advised port to PlayStation™ in 1999.

Bushnell and Baer's fortunes have differed over the years. Baer invented handheld electronic game *Simon* in 1978, the same year Bushnell was ousted from Atari after its sale to Warner Communications. Baer also invented the first ever light gun game as well as a talking doormat; Bushnell is currently incorporating videogame technology into a chain of restaurants across the US.

Between them, they built an industry, an empire. As such, *Pong*, despite its simplicity, must certainly qualify as the most influential game of all time.

Play it now!

The most authentic way of enjoying *Pong* these days is on an original Atari or Binatone TV console, widely available on eBay. Numerous Java-based games exist on the Internet, which can be played for free.

Pro Evolution Soccer 5

Publisher:	Konami
Developer:	KCET
Platform:	PS2
Released:	1998

There was a time when Electronic Arts' FIFA series was so dominant in the football market that it seemed there'd never be another way. But slowly, surely, Konami's *Pro Evolution Soccer* series has taken up a position as FIFA's chief rival. More than that, it's the only choice for those who take their football seriously; those who regard the game as a punchout between triumph and tragedy, not just a series of backheels, twists and thirty-yard screamers into the top right corner.

Actually, there's a useful rule of thumb to distinguish between games that take football seriously and those that try and fool the player with ludicrous glamour and improbable skill. Is it possible to give the ball to your goalkeeper, run the length of the pitch beating all the opposition players with built-in tricks and by taking advantage of flaws in the AI, and then cap the magnificent run with a finish worthy of a top-flight striker? Though FIFA isn't nearly as guilty of this exaggerated play as it used to be, *Pro Evolution Soccer* takes a diametrically opposite approach to the sport. You can't just pick up the controller and expect to score a goal.

In fact, perhaps the only reason *Pro Evolution* isn't completely dominant is because it's so difficult. While FIFA eases you into a game which plays out in like an arcade game, *Pro Evolution*'s approach is something closer to a simulation. You can expect to play several matches without scoring a goal, trudging your way through multi-goal defeats, single-goal losses, and disheartening 0-0 draws. When the first goal does come it's likely to be clumsy, scrambled, ugly. But at least it's a goal, and it'll feel like the winner in a World Cup Final.

Eventually, *Pro Evolution*'s approach will start to sit naturally with you. Like football itself, it's as much about what happens off the ball as on it, and learning where your teammates are going to run when you're in possession (and directing them by using the game's malleable tactics system) is key to breaking down opposition defences. It might be difficult at first, but when you've mastered it playing a well-timed through ball that bisects the opposition defence becomes as satifying as scoring a goal. And so *Pro Evolution Soccer* has these miniature moments of euphoria throughout the match, even though the numbers of goals scored remains realistically low.

It's impossible to approximate all the subtlety in football down to the buttons on a Dualshock, but there are still a great number of techniques to master in *Pro Evolution*. Every important part of football has some kind of analogue here, and each of these analogues has a difficulty curve that allows the player to improve their skill: management, tactics, dribbling, tackling, shooting; you can even get better at running off the ball once you've mastered the button that lets you break from the AI's predefined paths.

So, for example, you start by using the X button to pass, playing simple balls to teammates. It's not long before you graduate to circle, which allows you to the cross the ball. Then after some time while you learn to use triangle, which plays an automatic through ball that ends up at the feet of the opposition unless used with precise timing. It's a good number of hours beyond that before you'll even attempt to get to grips with analogue passing, which uses the right analogue stick on the PS2 to put a ball anywhere you want, regardless of whether there's a player there or not.

Though the management aspect mentioned above is hardly as comprehensive as a dedicated managment game (such as Eidos' *Championship Manager*, Sega's *Football Manager*, or Konami's own *Pro Evolution Manager*), its somewhat reductive nature allows players to make the key important decisions while being aware that success or failure will ultimately come down to their own footballing skill. This mode is called The Master League, and it's agony and ecstasy.

In the Master League you manage a team off the pitch as well as on. You buy players and you sell them, you train youngsters and manage your finances. It takes a very long time to make progress in the Master League, and over the time it's likely you'll become very attached to your team and the group of players you've built up. That, obviously, acts as a kind of enjoyment multiplier; you feel every victory and every defeat. Having put several months of effort in to make it to a situation where you're in the equivalent of the European Cup final, losing your star striker the game before with an injury and then losing the actual match to an 89th-minute wonder goal…

Sometimes *Pro Evolution Soccer* doesn't seem fair. And perversely that's what makes it like real football, what makes it better than all its rivals. Sure, FIFA has all the correct player details, the stadia, the competitions and the stylings. It has the glamour, the glitz and the goals. But *Pro Evolution Soccer* has the football.

Perhaps the only reason
Pro Evolution isn't
completely dominant is
because it's so difficult

Replay

□ Save   ✕ View   START End   SELECT Ctrl

□ Save   ✕ View   START End   SELECT Ctrl

□ Save   ✕ View   START End   SELECT Ctrl

KONAMI KONAMI KONAMI KONAMI KONAMI

Elapaed Time   Cleared
0'33"36   22

Play it now!

Pro Evolution Soccer 5 is Konami's latest and
greatest version, released at the end of 2005 and
readily available in shops. Versions of the series are
also available for the PSP™, Xbox and (shortly) the
Nintendo DS.

Resident Evil™ 4

Publisher:	Capcom
Developer:	Capcom Production Studio 4
Platform:	GameCube, PlayStation® 2
Released:	2005

Don't be fooled by the name – *Resident Evil 4* is actually the sixth title in the *Resident Evil* series, and that excludes spin-offs such as the *Outbreak* and *Gun Survivor* games. The core series has been critically and commercially acclaimed for over a decade now, selling over 30 million copies in total. But it's *Resident Evil 4* which stands head and shoulders above its peers. At last count it had received over 70 gaming awards worldwide – far more than any game in the series.

First released in 1996, *Resident Evil* (*Biohazard* in Japan) was a videogame with clear cinematic aspirations. Borrowing every zombie cliché from the Big Book Of Zombie Cliches, it dragged survival horror kicking and screaming into the next generation with a tale of a renegade corporation, a mysterious and deadly virus and monsters. Lots of monsters. And dogs.

Despite the increased technology offered by the PlayStation®, the game's design was nonetheless limited by the format, though the development team did their best to hide any shortcomings. Loading was a problem, but this was disguised by a slow door animation, which actually added to the tension. The environments could not be rendered with sufficient detail in realtime 3D; instead, static backgrounds were created – which, in turn, allowed more imaginative and atmospheric positioning of the stationary camera.

It was a global success, despite the fact that playing the game was an uncomfortable experience. Genuinely terrifying throughout, it hinted at the new gaming possibilities offered by the 32bit consoles, and the sequels *Resident Evil 2* and *Resident Evil 3: Nemesis* extended the series without altering too much. Despite being spin-offs – that is, existing outside of the main story arc – *Code Veronica* and *Zero* stuck rigidly to the now familiar *Resident Evil* experience.

But by *Nemesis*, it was fairly obvious the series was beginning to tire – despite the fact that zombies were enjoying a resurgence across the

board, from games to films and everything in between. For *Resident Evil* to retain its position at the top of the dead food chain, a fresh approach was needed.

Few could have predicted how radically the series would alter with *Resident Evil 4* – and even fewer could have predicted it would arrive on Game Cube initially. Where *Resident Evil* featured mostly slow, lumbering enemies, *RE4*'s opponents were smart, fast – and very aggressive. For the first time, the game moved into three full dimensions with a visual splendour few could believe, with this new perspective offering a complete freedom to move and fire anywhere.

And you'd need to. Enemies attacked with efficiency, using smart strategies. One of the game's stable tactics was immediately withdrawn. In previous *Resident Evil* titles, you could simply step through a door to escape any

aggressors, here, they'd break it down as part of the hunt. Dramatic set pieces maintained the ferocious pace, offering moments of peril impossible in previous games.

The series' trademark restrictive inventory was removed, making it easier to manage items, and the save system revamped. These were obvious concessions to modern games players who preferred more immediate action. Indeed, *Resident Evil 4* offered an abundance of ammunition with which to despatch these smarter enemies – a complete about-turn for the series.

Of course, the *Resident Evil* cognoscenti have debated these radical changes, some remaining so stubborn as to dismiss *Resident Evil 4*'s credibility on various internet forums. The wider world, though, embraced the game. It sold out its European allocation within weeks, and has amassed sales of over three million worldwide, including

the PlayStation® 2 port which followed months later. A fifth *Resident Evil* is in development, scheduled to appear on both PlayStation® 3 and Xbox 360.

There's little doubt that Capcom's re-imagining of the *Resident Evil* world paid huge dividends. It was an ambitious move – and one which could have spectacularly backfired had the design and implementation been anything short of perfect. Whilst clearly not for everyone – the gore is even more horrific, thanks to the increased graphical capabilities of both host formats – *Resident Evil 4* is, nonetheless, one of the greatest games you'll ever play, even if it doesn't look quite so pretty when viewed from behind your fingers. Certainly one of the best 50 games ever written. And on this evidence, the series based on the undead has much life in it yet.

Play it now!

Resident Evil 4 is widely available on both GameCube and PlayStation® 2. The latter is considered the more complete version, offering a host of unlockable extras which encourage repeat play.

Rez

Publisher: Sega/Sony Computer Entertainment
Developer: Sega – United Game Artists
Platform: Dreamcast, PlayStation® 2
Released: 2001

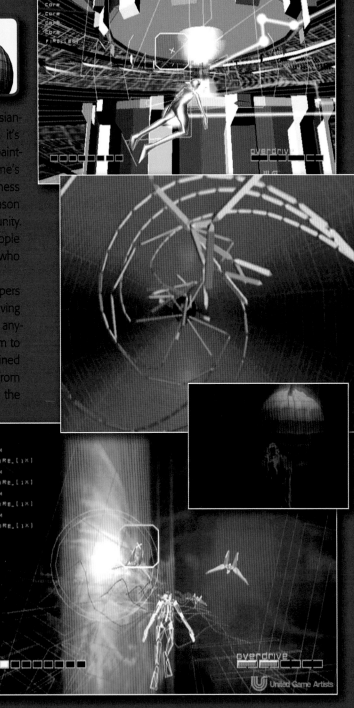

Rez is, simply, the finest ever rhythm-infused, Russian-painter-inspired, on-rails 3D-shoot 'em up. Sure, it's probably the only ever rhythm-infused, Russian-painter-inspired, on-rails 3D-shoot-'em-up, but in fact the game's sense of tripped-out originality and hallucinatory weirdness is a major part of its appeal. It's also probably the reason that the game divides the opinion of the gaming community. Because although it's an excellent game, and some people most certainly love it, there are, bizarrely, some people who don't.

It's almost possible to see why: while other developers were busy creating contemporary urban sandboxes and giving gamers the freedom to go anywhere and do (or shoot) anything or anyone, *Rez* put players on rails and limited them to shooting only those things they found in their predetermined path. In many ways it's got more in common with games from the 1980s, like *Afterburner* and *Space Harrier*, than with the polygonal epics of the PlayStation® era.

But the game is unlike both in a significant way. Although, at its heart, the game is a classic arcade shoot-'em-up, it takes its inspiration from a neurological condition known as synaesthesia – a mixing of the senses that actually occurs inside some people's brains, causing them to see sounds, or taste colours, and so on. Thus *Rez* layers evolving soundscapes on top of visually mutable environments to mimic the sensation of hearing colours and seeing sounds, and the result is a kaleidoscopically entrancing collision of action, sound and vision.

The game is the brainchild of Tetsuya Mizuguchi, then head of Sega's United Game Artists studio (and if you think too hard about the progression to *Rez* from his early titles like *Sega Rally* through the sci-fi groove of *Space Channel 5*, that's probably a

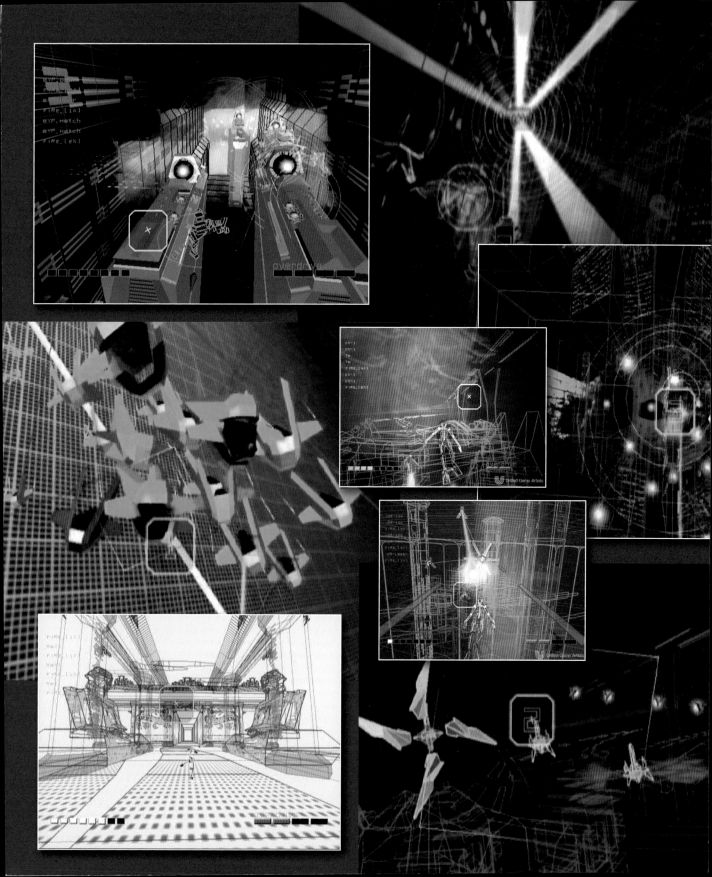

quite frightening insight into the inside of his brain). He dedicated the game to Russian painter Wassily Kandinsky and paid unofficial homage to the block-rocking beats of Underworld by naming it after one of their tunes (which also provided the soundtrack on early pre-release versions of the game, but couldn't accompany the finished product because of licensing problems).

A basic description of the game would go something like this: inside an abstract cyberspace, the player proceeds through five levels to save the central AI from a debilitating virus. The player's character travels into the screen on rails, with freedom only to dodge and aim at waves of attackers that arrive in predefined patterns. These attackers can be targeted individually, but the player also has a limited number of smart bombs and can lock on to up to eight enemies.

That, though, could describe countless 3D shoot-'em-ups. What distinguishes *Rez* is that a basic description simply doesn't do justice to the heady hallucinogenic brew dreamt up by Mizuguchi. His metamorphosing protagonist transmutes from wireframe amoeba to pulsing ball of transcendental energy if players perform well, and individual levels evolve from sparsely outlined abstractions to dizzyingly complicated visual edifices in synch with intensifying trance soundtracks. Pick off individual targets and they'll produce simple chimes – lock on and destroy increasing numbers of enemies and a more complex soundscape will emerge.

It reaches climax with the final and longest level, in which an exhilarating remix of Adam Freeland's *Fear* accompanies a sprawling journey through exotic structures that materialise out of constantly shifting alien landscapes before collapsing into the void. A series of final boss encounters then revisit the stunning set-pieces at the end of each previous level, ranging from deadly lotus leaves to a colossal, running man, who fades in and out of tangibility.

It's a perfect and fitting end to a breathtaking overall experience, but it's not all *Rez* has to offer. The action continues with a variety of extra modes and unlockables, including ever more mesmerising visual schemes and an invulnerable mode that essentially turns the game into a glorified light show. Oh, and in his desire to recreate the sensation of standing next

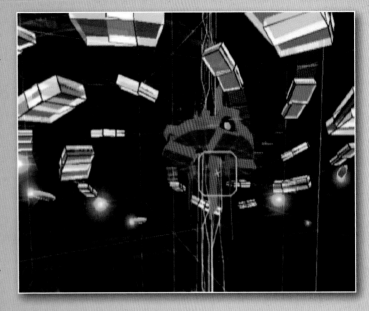

to a bass bin, Mizuguchi came up with the Trance Vibrator – a special peripheral that rumbles in time to the on-screen action. It quickly acquired internet infamy thanks to a few personal accounts by females who put it to a rather more intimate (mis)use than Mizuguchi had presumably originally envisaged.

Erotic peripherals aside, *Rez* is paradoxically a game that harks back to the simplicity of the pre-PlayStation® era while simultaneously looking forward. When Sony launched the PlayStation® 2, they did so with a series of adverts which described it as 'the third place' – a surreal, weirdly dreamlike, virtual space. More than any other game, *Rez* encapsulates this indistinct, vague notion of an alternative reality. It's a game that transports you to new imaginative vistas. And it's a game that's hugely satisfying and entertaining.

Play it now!

The Dreamcast version of *Rez* is now difficult to get hold of unless you're willing to pay a lot of money for a second-hand copy. The PlayStation® 2 version is less so, but you're still more likely to find a preowned copy than a brand new version – even in spite of its recent reissue in North America.

Ridge Racer™

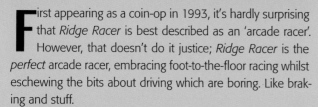

Publisher: Namco Limited
Developer: Namco Limited
Platform: Arcade
Released: 1993

First appearing as a coin-op in 1993, it's hardly surprising that *Ridge Racer* is best described as an 'arcade racer'. However, that doesn't do it justice; *Ridge Racer* is the *perfect* arcade racer, embracing foot-to-the-floor racing whilst eschewing the bits about driving which are boring. Like braking and stuff.

Forget *Gran Turismo*-style tinkering, tedious licence tests and the cone challenges in *Gotham*; *Ridge Racer* makes outrageous demands of the accelerator, fusing it to the floor whilst melting the steering column. The modern interpretation of *Ridge Racer* may as well do away with the brake entirely; speed starts, power slides and bursts of nitrous are the controls of choice.

At its heart, *Ridge Racer* is a by-the-numbers driving game. Start at the back of the grid and work your way into the top three positions by the end of the race. Do so, and move on. Don't, and it's game over. Simple.

The major difference with *Ridge Racer*, however, is its complete disregard for real-world physics. It's possible to slide round a hairpin at 100 miles per hour, maintaining the speed into, round and out of the corner. Crashing into other cars results in no visible damage; vehicles can be neatly shunted if they obstruct the racing line. It's hardly realistic, but it's much more fun than some of the po-faced racers which populate the market.

Cars vary in acceleration, top speed and handling but overall the style of racing never changes. Statistically, players are as likely to spend as much time sliding sideways than with their noses pointed in the direction of travel – it's an acquired taste for sure, but when it clicks there is no better racing game in the world.

Whilst these are similar in spirit, Ridge Racer *didn't originally look this pretty. These shots are from the most recent iteration:* Ridge Racer 6 *on Xbox 360.*

The original arcade game was set entirely in the fictional Ridge City. Just one course – with two variations – was on offer, with the difficulty spike coming thanks to faster cars rather than more demanding courses. Over the years, additional areas of Ridge City have been introduced to sate home rather than arcade gamers. The latest version on Xbox 360 boasts a seemingly endless supply of different routes and challenges. It's fair to say that few will ever see all *Ridge Racer 6* has to offer.

Ridge Racer 6, in all its reflective glory.

The appearance of *Ridge Racer 6* so early in the life of Xbox 360 was something of a coup for Microsoft as the game has become something of a launch talisman for the PlayStation® formats. When the home console first appeared in Japan in 1994, *Ridge Racer* best illustrated the power of the console, bringing arcade racing into homes like never before. *Ridge Racer V* was among the first titles released for PlayStation® 2 six years later. On PlayStation® Portable, a revamped *Ridge Racer* was available at launch. Of course, it would be churlish to suggest the consoles' subsequent success was completely due to *Ridge Racer*, but it's a good omen for Xbox 360. *Ridge Racer* has always proved a showcase for new hardware.

The series has always boasted a sense of fun. From the outrageous full-size Eunos Roadster which players sat in when playing *Ridge Racer Full Scale* in arcades, to the ridiculously fantastic craft which appear in the latter stages of *Ridge Racer 6*, it's a game which is meant to be played with a smile on the face. Moments of joy are never far from the course. Whether they're spectacular jumps offering stunning views across Ridge City or the incidental background detail such as planes taking off, helicopters tracing the action or luscious waterfalls cascading over some distant hill, it's a game which is a joy to behold – though admiring the scenery is something probably best saved for the replays rather than during the race.

It was the PSP™ title which provided perhaps the most controversial moment of the series with the introduction of nitrous speed boosts, dramatically altering the fundamentals of *Ridge Racer*. The series has always included elastic artificial intelligence – the cars typically 'bunch' together whatever the player performance – and nitrous boosts only amplified this. It was practically impossible to tear ahead and leave opponents for dust; one poorly taken corner would usually result in being overtaken, no matter how great the lead. Whilst this wasn't strictly speaking realistic, it did, however, make for endlessly thrilling races right up to the line.

Overall, though, *Ridge Racer* has remained largely the same since its introduction. Familiar cars, courses, and same emphasis on drift racing – little has changed from arcade to Xbox 360. Even the Japanese techno soundtrack is rooted firmly in the mid nineties, much to the annoyance of many audiophiles.

But turn the music down and the engine roar up and *Ridge Racer* on whatever format is a racing game like no other. A game whose popularity transcends the hardware, its enduring appeal illustrates that a fine racing game can rarely be bettered. And there are few finer than *Ridge Racer*.

Ridge Racer *on PSP™, the original game in handheld form – with a few tweaks and additions here and there.*

Play it now!

Ridge Racer 6 on Xbox 360 is by far the most complete version of *Ridge Racer* currently available. Even the nitrous boosts can be switched off, so purists can enjoy the original courses in high definition. Surprisingly, even the recently released mobile phone version impresses visually – though is let down by awkward controls. A PlayStation® 3 version of *Ridge Racer* is currently in development.

Ridge Racer™ © NAMCO BANDAI Games Inc.

Sid Meier's Civilization II

Publisher: Microprose
Developer: Microprose
Platform: PC, PlayStation®, Mac
Released: 1996

When *Sid Meier's Civilization II* was released, in 1996, other developers were creating ice and lava levels for plumbers to run around in, or caves and tombs for well-stacked posh girls with guns. So *Civilization II* was quite a bit of a contrast. It occupied itself with a rather more ambitious subject matter: nothing less than the sum of human history. In contrast to the parochial preoccupations of other games, *Sid Meier's Civilization II* attempted to provide the ultimate sandbox: the whole scope of human endeavour, encompassing history, philosophy, science, art, and, well, all of civilisation, basically. In doing so it created the computer gaming equivalent of crack cocaine: to players unable to stop playing in the bleary-eyed early hours, the march of progress proved quite literally unstoppable.

The game was a sequel to the original *Sid Meier's Civilization*, based by creator Sid Meier on a board game of the same name. Like its predecessor, it placed players at the head of an entire empire, and gave them the task of conquering the world against computer opposition, but it refined many of the underlying mechanics and replaced the blocky top-down visuals of the original with an attractive isometric representation of the world. It built on themes developed by Meier in his earlier game *Railroad Tycoon*, which he explored further in *Colonization* (both games focused on more limited time scales: a century in the case of the former; the colonisation of the New World from 1492 till 1850 in the case of the latter). And although it was graphically eclipsed by two further

sequels and various clones (including Meier's own *Alpha Centauri* and Activision's *Call to Power* series), it's *Sid Meier's Civilization II* that provides the most balanced and memorable gameplay.

Which is quite an achievement given the daunting scope and scale of the game. Players can choose from over 20 different civilisations, from the Aztecs and Babylonians to the English and French. Other starting races include the Celts, Greeks, Indians, Japanese, Romans, Vikings and Zulus. Over the course of the game there are around 90 technologies for players to discover, including political philosophies such as monarchy and feudalism, early discoveries such as alphabet and the wheel, and technologies that have shaped the world as we know it today: medicine, electricity,

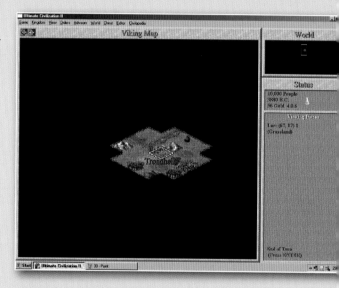

flight, nuclear power and genetic engineering. And then there are over 45 different types of military unit to play with: from archers and pikemen through musketeers to marines and paratroopers and then to cruise missiles and nuclear missiles.

A game so dizzyingly large and complicated could easily be overwhelming, but *Sid Meier's Civilization II* unfolds with a beguiling simplicity. The game starts with the player in control of just one group of settlers, used to create the game's first settlement. Early turns are then spent building an infrastructure, exploring the surrounding area, and learning the basics of civic improvements, scientific

Domestic Advisor

The population of the fertile Fujiwara empire now exceeds 1,000,000 citizens.

OK

Science Advisor

I recommend we develop The Republic so that we can someday learn: Banking.

Science Advisor

I recommend we develop Medicine so that we can build: Shakespeare's Theatre.

Military Advisor

We should build Paratroopers to surprise our enemies.

Domestic Advisor

Let us undertake a great project for the glory of our civilization, Hanging Gardens!

79, OBJECTIVE (T...

Citizens

City Resources

Food: 30   Surplus: 2

Trade: 8   Corruption: 0

80% Tax: 24   0% Lux: 0   20% Sci: 3

Change

What discovery shall our wise men pursue?

	Engineering
	Medicine
	The Republic
	Seafaring
	Theology
	University

| Help | Goal | OK |

What shall we build in Perm?

Engineers	(2 Turns, ADM: 0/2/2 HP: 2/1)
Partisans	(2 Turns, ADM: 4/4/1 HP: 2/1)
Alpine Troops	(2 Turns, ADM: 5/5/1 HP: 2/1)
Riflemen	**(2 Turns, ADM: 5/4/1 HP: 2/1)**
Marines	(2 Turns, ADM: 8/5/1 HP: 2/1)
Paratroopers	(2 Turns, ADM: 6/4/1 HP: 2/1)
Mech. Inf.	(2 Turns, ADM: 6/6/3 HP: 3/1)
Armor	(3 Turns, ADM: 10/5/3 HP: 3/1)
Howitzer	(3 Turns, ADM: 12/2/2 HP: 3/2)
Fighter	(2 Turns, ADM: 4/3/10 HP: 2/2)
Bomber	(4 Turns, ADM: 12/1/8 HP: 2/2)
Helicopter	(4 Turns, ADM: 10/3/6 HP: 2/2)
Cruise Msl.	(2 Turns, ADM: 18/0/12 HP: 1/3)

| Auto | Help | OK |

Map | Rename

w | Exit

Resc

Unite S

City Imp

Temple
MarketPlac
City Walls
Aqueduct
Bank
Cathedral
University
Colosseum
Factory

Start | Ultimate Civilization II | 4 - Paint   22:22

Ultimate Civilization II

Game Kingdom View Orders Advisors World Cheat Editor Civilopedia

Norman Map

Inverness

Aberdeen

World

Status

1,970,000 People
Feb 1066
d 4.1.5

Viewing Pieces

, 55) 7
nd)

Edinburgh (Scottish and Welsh OBJECTIVE city)

Demands Copper, Beads, and Spice.

| OK |

Carlisle

FOREIGN MINISTER - Intelligence Report
Emperor Alexius Comnenus of the Byzantine Greeks (Uncooperative, Allied)
Militaristic

Government: Monarchy   Capital: Constantinople
Treasury: 309 Gold Military: 21 Units   Researching: Invention

ALLIED with King William II of the English Normans
ALLIED with King Bohemund of the Italians and Normans
At PEACE with King Henry IV of the Germans
ALLIED with King Phillip I of the French and Burgundians
At WAR with Sultan Barkiyarok of the Seljuk Turks
CONTACT with Caliph al-Mustali of the Fatimid Egyptians

Alphabet	Code of Laws	Feudalism
Bridge Building	Construction	Horseback Riding
Bronze Working	Currency	Iron Working
Ceremonial Burial	**Engineering**	Literacy
Special Technology	Special Technology	Map Making

| Cities | Close |

End of Turn
(Press RETURN)

Texcoco, 1680 B.C.

Ultimate Civilization II

Game Kingdom View Orders Advisors World Cheat Editor Civilopedia

Food Storage

City of Aldrin, N.B. 14 (Treasury: 25 Gold)

Citizens   City Resources

Populatio   Surplus

Trade: 2   Corruption

50% Tax: 1 0% Lux: 0   50% Sci

Resource Map

Buy | Change

Units Support: 9   Production: 2

City Improvements

Caravan

Tlatelolco builds Caravan. What trade goods shall it carry?

- ● Hides
- ○ Copper
- ○ Silk
- ○ Food Supplies

Supply And Demand	OK

Aztec High Council

Military	Science	Trade	Foreign	Attitude

Attitude: We should raise the luxury rate

Cancel

Receptive Japanese Emissary

"We have prepared a permanent peace treaty confirming the friendship between our two peoples and fixing our mutual borders for all time. Will you sign it?"

- ● "Yes, we welcome peace with the Japanese."
- ○ "No, your terms are not acceptable."

OK

=The Situation=

Six governments established bases on Mars. Working together, they managed to convert large portions of the Martian polar ice caps into a useable water supply.

Just as they were poised to begin the next step, something went wrong back home. Communications ceased without warning, even navigational telemetry from the Mars orbiters stopped. Assuming the worst--a major war, the end of civilization, or both--the colonists succumbed to irrationality. Contact between the six bases was cut off, and attitudes have grown cold.

Dissident humans who believe that communications were cut off intentionally have revolted and set up their own base. They refer to themselves as "Martians".

As leader of one of the bases, you have a choice. You can seek to conquer your neighbors and unify Mars by force, or you can strive to regain contact with Earth and find out what happened. Good luck!

OK

Icy Hojo Emissary

"Your civilization makes us laugh. We will agree not to crush your worthless civilization in exchange for the secret of Monastery Const.."

- ● "We ignore your hollow threats."
- ○ Give secret of Monastery Const..

OK

Defense Minister

Our alliance with the Byzantine Greeks has been cancelled. All of our units in Byzantine territory have been relocated to our nearest cities; Byzantine units in our territory have been similarly relocated.

OK

Forest

Move Cost:	2	Effect of Engineer Transformation:
Unit Defense Bonus:	+50%	Grassland
Food:	1	Effects of Roads:
Shields:	2	Move Cost: 1/3 of a point
Trade:	0	Possible Resources:
Effects of Irrigation:	Plains	Pheasant
Turns to Irrigate:	5	Silk
Effects of Mining:	(N/A)	
Turns to Mine:	5	

Go Back	Description	Close

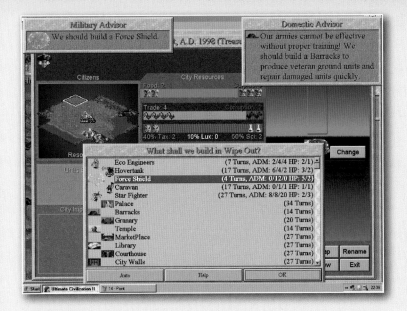

discoveries, diplomacy and economics. From here, the game blossoms down ever more complex avenues as players create more cities and discover the rest of the world; making war or diplomacy, discovering technologies and the Wonders of the World, and ultimately, in 200 turns, conquering every other civilisation, or building a spaceship to reach Alpha Centauri.

Along the way, it's possible to take advice from a High Council of advisors, customise your throne room and keep your citizens happy with generous tax schemes and city improvements like city walls, universities, factories, cathedrals and police stations. A utopian element is also apparent as players contend with problems that continue to perplex modern governments – solving pollution by discovering sources of energy such as hydro and solar power, and discovering the cure for cancer, for example. The latter is one of several unique Wonders that have beneficial effects across a civilisation's entire population. Others include the Hanging Gardens of Babylon, Michaelangelo's Chapel, the Statue of Liberty and (perhaps optimistically) the SETI Program.

Apart from the sheer addictive joy of making new discoveries, one of the defining features of the game is its historical interest: it's actually a philosophically interesting game that has inspired commentary from academics, such as one anthropologist who questioned the game's use of particularly American assumptions about historical progress. Certainly, although it presents players with the freedom to make their own choices, the game is clearly (and perhaps inevitably) based on certain

suppositions about the ideal society. Nevertheless, it still provides an amusing opportunity to investigate various ahistorical what ifs, particularly with regard to combat match ups, such as Greek phalanxes fighting European musketeers, or US Marines contending with old world catapults.

It's just one more factor contributing to the enduring success of the game, further cemented through various add-ons and expansions which introduced multiplayer competition and fantastic settings. Ultimately though, it is the addictive, highbrow, cerebral structure of the game that makes it so endearing – and proving the enormous reach of videogames and the depth and scope of the medium.

Play it now!

Sid Meier's Civilization II has been followed by two official sequels: Sid Meier's Civilization III and Sid Meier's Civilization IV. All three games are currently available to buy for the PC. Several spin-offs and unofficial sequels, such as Sid Meier's Alpha Centauri, Civilization: Call to Power and Call to Power II, are also available. There are even several freeware games inspired by the Civilization series, which can be downloaded from the internet and played for free – such as Freeciv and C-evo – but the original games rights are currently owned by US publisher, Take 2.

Screens are reproduced courtesy of Firaxis Games.

The Sims™

Publisher:	Electronic Arts
Developer:	Maxis
Platform:	PC
Released:	2000

Yuppie mating rituals, part one: dirty putting talk

There are few titles that can claim to have broken gaming's traditional demographics as effectively as *The Sims*. In a gaming market that is almost always dominated by males, it became the number one selling game of all time by focusing on a gaming dynamic that didn't exclude anyone. In fact, creator Will Wright – the man behind another genre-busting title, *Sim City* – calls *The Sims* a 'digital dollhouse', a phrase that while describing the gameplay almost perfectly, isn't the sort of term marketing men in a pre-*Sims* age would like to hear.

But Will Wright hasn't ever been interested in producing games that appeal to pre-formed demographics. *The Sims* arose through experimentation, Wright playing around with the idea of producing an architecture simulation. The people who would eventually form the focus of the title were only included as tests for the architecture. But people love people, not bricks, and Electronic Arts will be forever grateful the game's selling point shifted from construction of buildings to construction of lives.

In *The Sims* you have a character, a Sim, and you have a house. The idea is to make your Sim's life as comfortable as possible. In Sim terms, comfort is measured with consumerism, the perfect digital commentary on the American Dream. A bigger house, a better television, a higher income, a more beautiful partner; all of these things can be yours, assuming you manage to live your life to the highest standard possible.

You achieve this by balancing a number of energy bars. The energy bars represent eight different things, labelled Bladder, Hunger, Energy, Comfort, Hygiene, Social, Fun and Room. To keep the bladder bar low you need to go to the toilet a lot, and to keep the hunger bar low you need to eat a lot. Keeping energy high requires lots of sleep or coffee, while watching TV or sitting down will increase your Sim's comfort. Hygiene means cleaning your Sim regularly; having a bath and washing your hands after going to the toilet. Similar to

CREATE A CHARACTER

PERSONALITY

Neat
Outgoing
Active
Playful
Nice

Points Remaining

DONE   CANCEL

APPEARANCE

Maria

BIO

Maria Gonzales left SimCity because the mayor just couldn't keep crime levels low. She's much more happy in the suburbs and just got a new entry level job at Now that she has time to study, she

CREATE A SIM

PERSONAL   DONE

STYLE
HAT

STYLE

ACCEPT   BACK

CREATE A SIM

PERSONAL   BODY   DONE

FACE STYLE

HAIR/HAT
COLOR

FACIAL HAIR

EYE COLOR

ACCESSORIES

ACCEPT   BACK

CREATE A SIM

PERSONAL   BODY   DONE

FACE STYLE

HAIR/HAT
COLOR

ACCEPT   BACK

CREATE A SIM

BODY   DONE

EYE COLOR

ACCESSORIES

ACCEPT   CANCEL

You need a few lessons from the artist next door, mate

comfort, fun means keeping your Sim entertained, and social governs their interaction with other Sims. Room is a measure of how attractive your Sim's current surroundings are — which is where the architecture element comes in, and why you'll want to spend your hard-earned currency on new objects for your Sim's beloved home.

It all seems faintly ridiculous, but then it's a videogame, and as simplified extrapolations of how the human race measures success go, it isn't bad. You spend your life juggling tasks you have to do and tasks you want to do, maybe trying to maintain your climb up the social strata, maybe trying to find a bigger house and to fill it with beautiful things, maybe just trying to be happy. The main difference between that way of living and *The Sims* is that you don't have the physical manifestations of your various states of happiness as energy bars. Or the green diamond above your head, one assumes.

Of course, that's only one way of playing the game; what tips sections in videogames magazines might consider the correct way, but that's likely to be as far, far away from what many people do with the game. See, it's just as much fun to take Will Wright's digital dollhouse and play with it as if it were a sandbox of humanity. Freed from the irons of virtual conformity, suddenly the possiblities seem endless. Create the perfect couple

This is what happens when you peel and iron an Austrian

196

and then throw a third perfect person into the mix. Use it as a social demonstration to see what happens when someone works without play, plays without work. Make your Sim's life try and match your own, then change some circumstances and see how he or she reacts. Marvel as you watch yourself playing on a computer in a game you're playing on a computer, circumstance reflected to infinity in a digital hall of mirrors. It's not exaggerating to say at times *The Sims* seems less like a game, more like an art-house installation.

But just to underline the fact that this isn't a piece of obscure virtual esoteria, we should restate its success again: *The Sims* is the best selling computer game of all time. Just because girls weren't buying games didn't mean they didn't want to buy them, and so Wright proved. *The Sims* didn't just sell millions of copies on its own, but spawned no less than seven expansion packs. Those expansion packs might have been increasingly desperate as time went on (*Superstar* turned your Sims into digital celebrities, while *Makin' Magic* gave them the ability to use magic and cast spells), stretching the credulity as much as the wallet, but it's not like *The Sims* didn't push more important boundaries elsewhere. And that's why it's in this list; not because it's the best selling game of all time, but because for millions of people who wouldn't otherwise be gamers, it's the only game that matters.

Play it now!

As well as the many budget-priced compilations of the original *The Sims* and its many add-on packs, *The Sims 2* is a logical expansion of the franchise on PC. If you've only got a console then there are versions of the game on most systems, albeit usally with a slightly simplified take on the virtual life concept.

Soulcalibur™ II

Publisher: Electronic Arts/Nintendo
Developer: Namco
Platform: Arcade, PlayStation® 2, Xbox, GameCube
Released: 2002

'Welcome, to the stage of history!' booms the histrionic voiceover at the start of each *Soulcalibur* – the perfectly bombastic introduction to a positively brash beat-'em-up, featuring bright, bold visuals, colourful characters, sexy girls, big weapons, and – in a novelty for the genre – an actual, honest-to-goodness singleplayer game beyond just the basic eight rounds of arcade combat. Battering the competition out of the way with its accessible combos and genuine 3D movement, its own place in history was assured when the first game in the series became only the second game ever to receive a perfect 40/40 score from the legendary (and notoriously mean) Japanese gaming magazine *Famitsu*.

Although its predecessor, *Soul Edge*, had proved relatively popular, *SoulCalibur* originally received an underwhelming reception when it was released in Japanese arcades. But it benefited from a renewed lease of life thanks to an astonishingly impressive conversion for Sega's new Dreamcast console. *Soulcalibur II* maintains this trajectory of cutting-edge technical achievement, along with its innovative hallmark fighting features.

Most notably these included an accessible and forgiving control system: although this is appealing to newcomers, it doesn't preclude the levels of complexity expected by hardcore fans obsessed with arcane intricacies like 'frame advantages' and 'combo buffering' (fancy terms describing the timing of combo-attacks used by more experienced gamers to confuse novices). By adding weapons to a genre that more usually featured hand-to-hand combat, the series introduced a new layer of tactical nuance: the range of characters and their attacks took on a new significance, which was further

accentuated by full 3D movement (or '8-Way Run' as Namco called it). A subtle blocking and counter-attacking system rounded out the core mechanics, along with special Soul Charge moves (which inflict increased damage on an opponent) and Spirit Charge manoeuvres (which are unblockable).

Equally importantly, *Soulcalibur II* preserves the breathtaking visuals of its predecessor. Arenas are bursting with background detail and vibrant colour: cherry blossom, lava moats and castle battlements all add atmosphere, and the game's vividly rendered combatants, meanwhile, engage each other with gymnastic grace and a carefully graded set of moves. These range from the cumbersome damage dealing of giant-axe-wielders to the acrobatic evasions of nimble ninjas, and are fleshed out with outlandish biographical detail: Astaroth, for example, is an automaton created by the god of war, who takes his name from the Duke of Hell and wields an enormous axe. Cervantes is an undead pirate and father to the graceful Ivy, who in turn is an aristocratic alchemist wielding a whip-like snake sword (and a character frequently used by top competition players). Or there's Voldo, a leather-bound blind catamite, next to whom the staff-wielding Kilik seems really rather ordinary. As for Sophitia, who looks more suited to ancient Greece than medieval Europe: let's face it, in a game featuring giant-axe-wielding golems and noblewomen alchemist daughters of undead pirates, who's going to care about a little anachronism?

One feature unique to *Soulcalibur II* is that it rounds out its character roster with three platform-specific fighters: Heihachi Mishima, better known for his appearances

Mummy, that lady makes my trousers feel funny

in the *Tekken* series; Link, better known for being an elf and saving princesses; and *Spawn*, better known as the comic-book creation of Todd McFarlane (who was also responsible for an underwhelming new character called Necrid who is probably better left unmentioned).

The game's background character narratives are, by beat-'em-up standards (and perhaps appropriately for a game set in the sixteenth century), Shakespearean in their complexity, which is another feature that has drawn fans to the series. More notable than the sentient-but-malignant sword from which the game takes its name is the way the stories of each of the different characters intertwine on their path to secure it for themselves – and the plot also benefits from a bit of Jacobean-style bloodshed as a broadsword-brandishing knight named Siegfried carries out a killing spree across Europe for three years.

Significantly though, this Byzantine narrative arc is used as a framing device for *Soulcalibur*'s greatest innovation: an extended singleplayer campaign, bestowing the game with a hugely satisfying learning curve and unlocking an unprecedented multitude of extras, from concept and promotional artwork to new costumes and weapons. Its most significant characteristic is that it gradually introduces players to the various subtleties that lie beneath the surface of the game's ostensibly simple interface.

Thus, while early missions simply require players to perform basic manoeuvres, later missions force them to fight in the face of various different constraints: using certain moves to avoid sinking through the floor, for example, or dispatching a certain number of opponents with particular types of attack.

It's a feature that many games have tried to emulate, but none have really equalled. Indeed while its paradigmatic impact might not be so obvious today next to the superficial beauty of so many next-gen beat-'em-ups, *Soulcalibur II* remains unequalled in substance. It remains to this day one of the outstanding examples of the genre.

Play it now!

Soulcalibur II is still available to play on Xbox, PlayStation® 2 and GameCube. It has also recently been followed up by *Soulcalibur III*, released only on the PlayStation® 2.

Space Invaders

Publisher: Midway
Developer: Taito Corporation
Platform: Arcade
Released: 1978

Before *Space Invaders*, arcade games players had no lives. Literally. Prior to the release of Taito's first coin-op, videogames were governed by a specific amount of time rather than a set number of tries. Changing this in one fell swoop was a bold move – yet it was a design feature which proved highly influential, changing the landscape and structure of games from that period on.

On its release in 1978, *Space Invaders* was an instant success – even commonly credited with being responsible for a shortage of Yen coins in its native Japan. In America, teenagers even took to begging on the streets for

quarters. The grown-ups, of course, were not impressed.

The game was created by designer Toshihiro Nishikado and programmer David Yuh. Their goal was to replicate the popular fairground shooting galleries in digital form, and keep its implementation wonderfully simple. H.G. Wells provided the inspiration for the look of the aliens – Nishikado admitted that the novel *War of the Worlds* and its description of the invading lifeforms shaped his initial designs for the game's primitive sprites.

Using either a two-directional joystick or left and right buttons – depending which version of the arcade cabinet they were using – players controlled a moveable laser

cannon, the last defence of Earth. Above, wave after wave of relentless aliens descended from the skies, tracing a convoluted route down towards the ground level. If an alien landed, it was Game Over. Periodically, a mothership would sweep across the top, offering random bonus points if destroyed. Aficionados soon worked out that there was nothing arbitrary about its bounty – the technology to generate a random number wasn't included in the game's hardware. To gain most points, players had to hit the mothership with their 23rd shot, and then every 15th thereafter. In a world obsessed by three-letter entries on high score tables, this kind of detail was important.

Four bases provided the player with shelter from the shower of laser beams, though these were degraded every time they were hit and frequently didn't last a level. No energy bars here – it was one shot, one kill for both sides. Tense stuff. Clear a wave of alien invaders, and a new one would appear, marching mercilessly towards the Earth's surface.

The period's limited technology required Nishikado to limit his ambitions in all areas of game design – whilst employing clever sleight-of-hand to paper over the primitive cracks. The most obvious change was in the enemies. Originally, the team considered designing a game based around shooting down planes – but they proved too complicated for the hardware to display.

Nishikado opted for alien invaders as the protagonists for the game because he felt the depiction of shooting human beings 'morally wrong'. His admirable stance –

long since abandoned by the modern games industry – inadvertently created gaming's most iconic of images, and its purist form of play remains as powerful and satisfying even today.

The original cabinet displayed black-and-white visuals only, but this was disguised by coloured Perspex strips applied to the machine's reflective screen to create waves of aliens in varying colours. Additionally, as the number of invading aliens decreased, so their acceleration increased, making it more difficult to pick off the remaining stragglers as they sped downwards. This was an interesting game design discovered by accident – when there were fewer aliens on screen, the processor could redraw them on screen much faster. The team decided to keep it in – no doubt encouraged by an increased difficulty curve resulting in more players failing. Insert another coin.

The success of *Space Invaders* brought a host of clones, some official, others blatant rip-offs. Other titles expanded on the ideas premiered in *Space Invaders* – *Galaxian* (1979) introduced more complicated attack formations, and *Phoenix* (1980) is credited with introducing the premise of a separate boss character.

Despite the fact it will soon enter its 30th year, *Space Invaders* remains one of the most popular games of all time, appearing in one form or other on almost every subsequent iteration of gaming technology. Predictably, by updating the game for modern consoles, latter-day designers overcomplicate the original design, destroying the essence of *Space Invaders*. It was never about 3D graphics, or special moves. Left-right-fire are all you ever need.

For many thirty-somethings, the introduction of the *Space Invaders* cabinet will mark the start of their passion for playing games – and many of those will continue to wear T-shirts adorned with the logo or artwork. Those too young to hang around in the arcades, chip shops and takeaways in the late seventies won't have the same affinity for the title – but it's a sure bet that everyone who has picked up a joystick, joypad or mouse to play a videogame will at some point have played *Space Invaders*.

Play it now!

Taito Legends for PlayStation® 2, Xbox and PC boasts a faithful conversion of the original *Space Invaders* and a couple of sequels, alongside many other classic Taito arcade games. Additionally, decent conversions of *Space Invaders* are available for the majority of mobile phones. *Space Invaders Evolution* for PSP™ includes a brilliant two-player head-to-head version of the original game along with an updated tribute which bizarrely includes rhythm action elements.

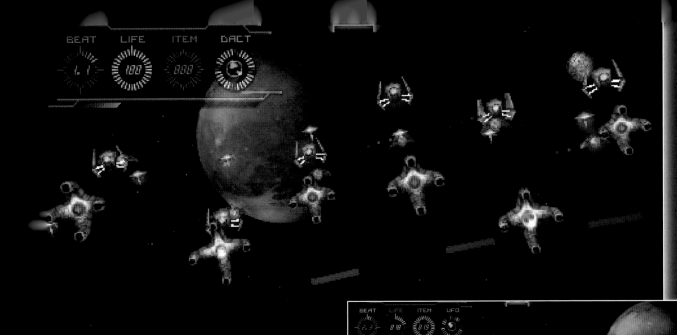

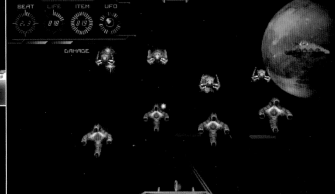

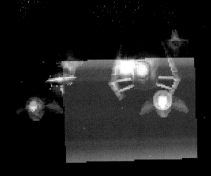

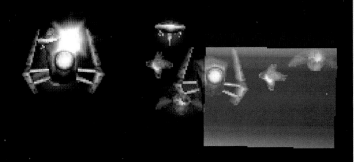

lution *on PSP™ retains the repetitive wave-*
e original game, albeit with 3D visuals.
rilliant competitive two-player version.

Street Fighter™ II

Publisher: Capcom
Developer: Capcom
Platform: Arcade
Released: 1991

I t's easy to forget just how big a deal *Street Fighter™ II* was back in the early nineties. Everyone talked about it, wanted it, had to have it right now. When it was released for the Super Nintendo and not, initially, the Sega Megadrive, pundits considered it a defining moment in that era's console war. They even made a movie based on

the game, remember? Back before Hollywood regularly plundered the games industry for intellectual property. And sure, it was awful. But still, they made a movie based on it, which was more than they did for most games. So what made *Street Fighter™ II*'s take on digitally brutalising another person so appealing? The answer: a lot of skill and a little luck.

Capcom's setup for street fighting is hardly revolutionary, similar to so many other fighting games before and since. You begin by selecting one of eight fighters and, depicted side-on with bright, beautiful pixels, you try to hit and kick your opponent more than they can hit and kick you. There are six buttons to attack with, and a joystick that lets you move your

Street Fighter™ III, *the true sequel to* **Street Fighter™**

Super Street
Fighter™ II

fighter left and right, jump and defend. If you win the fight you get to fight someone else, a different character from a different region of the globe with different special moves and slightly sharper AI. If you lose you get to insert a coin and try again, because that's how arcade games work.

How else arcade games work: by giving the gamer the kind of fast, adrenaline-laced entertainment that makes them want to play again. Fighting in *Street Fighter*™ is quick, fun and largely dependent on acid-quick reactions and nerves of steel. It is about having the sense to pick your moment; observing (and defending against) opponents' attack patterns, and being confident your sudden approach will provide you with a one or two frame window in their animation cycle in which to strike a crucial blow. Early on in your learning curve you'll find it doesn't, and you end up bruised, battered and dizzy.

Later even the toughest enemies succumb to your ruthless attack strategies, and the only place left to go is combat with another player. In two player battles, which perhaps predictably are *Street Fighter*™'s greatest strength, psychology plays a much bigger part. Your job becomes disguising your tactics and producing patterns in play that your (human) opponent can't second guess. At the same time you're calling them out on every move they make: high kick, low punch, special move.

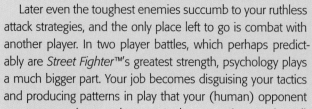

Certainly part of the reason for *Street Fighter*™'s appeal are those special moves. Normal attacks are performed by hitting one of eight different directions and six different fire buttons at the same time. Special moves require players to perform a fast sequence of button presses and produce a supernaturally effective attack. The most memorable of these is Ken and Ryu's fireball, executed by first circling the arcade stick (or d-pad, for console gamers) in a quarter circle towards your opponent, starting at the bottom and finishing with left and right, and then pressing punch. Quarter-circle-punch was almost as much of a mantra to 16-bit videogamers as the Konami cheatcode was to their 8-bit forefathers.

As well as the hugely satisfying special move system, *Street Fighter*™ *II* offered 'combos'. These unbreakable sequences of moves apparently arose via accident, a glitch in the code bringing about fast end-to-end chains of moves that it was impossible to defend against if the first blow had been landed, only noticed when the design team were watching slow-motion replays of demo fights. Regardless, it proved one of the game (and indeed the whole fighting game genre's) defining aspects. No longer was the skill limited to action and reaction, but also in crafting extended moves for yourself; coming up with unbreakable combos that, once they'd been started, could drop an opponent's energy to devastating effect.

At the time magazines printed lists of these combos, button sequences to learn that if executed correctly could turn a losing situation in your favour.

Cheat codes, essentially, but while most cheat codes have the potential to ruin the game they target, these ones only served to enhance it. The beauty of *Street Fighter*™ is that if both players are armed with the same knowledge, then both players know how to employ it and defend against it. Every fight is fair; that's the most important thing in VS fighting games, it always has been, always will be. That might as well be *Street Fighter*™ *II*'s unspoken motto, too, because it's always hard, always physical, always fair. And that's why – regardless of whether people can remember exactly how important the game was fifteen years ago – the spirit of Capcom's defining fighter will live on for many, many years.

Play it now!

There are sequels and derivatives of *Street Fighter*™ *II* available for most machines these days, the 'Alpha' series being particularly popular with a version recently released on PSP™. But perhaps the best way to experience Capcom's classic on a modern machine is through the Xbox Live Arcade edition, available on the Xbox 360.

Super Mario™ 64

Publisher: Nintendo
Developer: Nintendo
Platform: N64
Released: 1996

Everyone knows Mario. It seems like everyone's *always* known Mario. A short, stocky, cartoon plumber, as sweet and well-rounded as a kids' cartoon character, he was videogaming's first human-shaped icon. *Super Mario Bros* defined the platform game's simple formula: run fast from left to right, jump on the heads of cute creatures, and get to the goal before the time runs out. And while other companies tried to build on Nintendo's success, the only pixel person who managed to better Mario was, surprise, Mario.

The follow-ups were straight sequels, each increasing in sophistication and scale over the last. *Super Mario Bros 3* on the NES is still the most successful videogame of all time, selling 18 million copies. The Super Nintendo's *Super Mario World* is one of, if not the defining title of 16-bit early-nineties console gaming. But as Nintendo pushed at the limits of the genre, it soon became clear there were limits. There's only so much you can do with a two-dimensonal environment; only so many times players will buy into it. Where next?

The answer came thanks to a shift of perspective in gaming – but, at first at least, it didn't look like it would come from Nintendo. Though gamers had grown up with Mario, as the 3D age fell on gaming in the mid-nineties so Sony's PlayStation® was positioned as the true way forward for gamers wishing to enter this new dimension; to be the first virtual

explorers in these new worlds. Consoles were to provide virtual passports that would allow gamers to visit places they'd previously only seen side-on. It was to be a gaming revolution, and all eyes were on Sony.

Then Nintendo released the Nintendo64, dropped Mario into 3D, and everything changed: enter *Super Mario 64*.

The biggest worry was how gamers would react to a version of Mario that played in three dimensions. This was uncharted territory, after all. There were no rules for how 3D platform games would play, no other games to copy, no mistakes to learn from. All that was clear was that Mario would need

something more than just speed and judicious jumping to defeat Bowser this time. Nintendo settled on setting him the challenge of collecting stars hidden around a super cute castle, solving simple skill-based puzzles in toybox environments.

The adventure begins in the castle's primary-coloured gardens where Mario bursts out of one of the series' signature green pipes to greet players with a grin and a punch of the air. The control system was designed in tandem with the hardware on which it's played, and that perfect match of hardware and game design shows itself in every instant. Though it uses every button on the complex, oddly shaped N64 controller, the controls never feel overwhelming. The basics: the stick for movement, A to jump. That is all you need to worry about. Everything else comes later – and comes just as naturally. It always feels elegant, natural and responsive.

More importantly than that it also feels fun. Mario is an energetic, hyper-kinetic character, obvious from those first few seconds in the garden, but he is also very easily tamed. There is no painful learning curve in *Super Mario 64*, no dumbed-down tutorial levels, just seconds that turn into minutes as you potter around the grounds chasing butterflies, sliding down slopes and swimming in the moat. No quests are set until you make your way over the drawbridge and into the castle, but there is no rush, no pressure. Still fun today, the way Mario is controlled offers the most solid of foundations, a subtlety and delicacy that hasn't been bettered since.

Even with a perfect control system platforming in 3D is difficult, which is why the first few challenges in *Super Mario 64* are gentle affairs that allow much room for error. They're far removed from the previous Mario games' emphasis on pixel-perfect jumping and expert platforming. It's an experience that's far more about exploration and discovery than it

is reliant on timing and reaction. Sometimes it's fun just playing the tourist.

Not that *Mario 64* is an easy adventure, just an intelligent one. Completing it – defeating Bowser, rescuing Princess Peach and sitting back to watch the credits roll – will not tax most gamers, but managing to collect all of the castle's 120 stars is a badge of honour that anyone can wear with pride, requiring nothing less than complete mastery of every single arena. Solving the final quests requires traditional platform skills that are every bit as frustrating as those in, say, *Super Mario Bros 3*; but by this time you've spent so much time in the world that you feel part of it, feel the weight of the character with every jump. Even at the end the tasks are challenging rather than frustrating.

But back to the tourism: Mario enters those arenas, a blend of the comfortably recognisable and delightfully original, by diving through paintings hung in rooms inside the central castle. Most veterans of videogame travel will be familiar with the settings behind the parched dunes of Shifting Sand Land, its firey volcano-centred counterpart

Lethal Lava Land, and the ice-cool Cool Cool Mountain, a level which feels like a Christmas snowglobe. But the adventure also takes in the heartbreakingly hardcore sky platforming of Rainbow Road and the intricate internal clockwork mechanics of Tick Tock Clock, as well as Tiny-Huge Island, a world that makes a confounding puzzle out of perspective.

That delicious combination of innovation and familiarity was another thing that made *Super Mario 64* such an unstoppable proposition in 1996, and that turned Mario's creator, Shigeru Miyamoto, into videogaming's first real human icon. While the edge has been taken off his innovation by the hundreds of imitators since, the overall experience has never been bettered. It is not just that every single part of the game is magical, but that the game itself is somehow more than the sum of its parts; it's a theme park that's as fun to explore as it is to try and defeat, a perfect imaginary holiday destination. You can travel to a thousand different places in videogames and you might consider yourself a veteran, but if you haven't visited this version of the Mushroom Kingdom your passport might as well be empty, and if you don't know Mario – this Mario, the best Mario – then you should really make an effort to introduce yourself.

Play it now!

The best way is to find a second-hand N64, or wait for Nintendo's Revolution which may well offer the game through its online services. The other option is to look at the re-released version, a launch title for Nintendo's DS handheld system. Though the game suffers from being shoehorned into a format it wasn't designed for, the company eased the pain by adding a number of extra features. Thirty extra stars are hidden around the castle in the handheld version, and finding and catching bunny rabbits will unlock special touch-screen minigames designed to demonstrate the DS's unique capabilites. Perhaps most enticingly, *Super Mario 64* DS features a multiplayer mode which allows players to link machines and chase each other around Princess Peach's castle.

Super Mario™ 64 © 1997 Nintendo.

221

Super Monkey Ball

Publisher: Sega
Developer: Sega (Amusement Vision)
Platform: GameCube, arcade
Released: 2001

There are games in this book that are hugely complex in construction, and there are games that are elementary in design. There are games here that have been put together with target audiences in mind and some whose audience has arisen from nothing more than the brilliance of the idea. And there are games that take others' designs and improve upon them, and games that are wholly new ideas. The beauty of gaming is that it is broad enough to encompass all these philosophies and more; that spectacular entertainment can emerge from so many different concepts.

There is only one game in this book that was designed to be played with a controller shaped like a banana.

And gosh, what a gimmick that sounds like, what a terrible concept. But actually the game is more gimmick-free than a thousand other titles, so simple as to be completely elementary, almost wholly described by its title. In *Super Monkey Ball* you play a monkey in a ball. The ball rests at one end of a precarious maze, a hundred miles up in a classic videogame sky. To move the monkey you tip the maze, and the objective is to steer the ball to the other end of the

maze and to the goal within a time limit and without falling off the edge. Complete the level and you move up to the next. Fail, and you have to retry. That is it. That is the whole of *Super Monkey Ball*'s design, right there. The key point: that *Super Monkey Ball* is as simple as it is addictive.

Control is everything, and *Super Monkey Ball*'s control model is an analogue of the game design itself: simple, beautiful, as perfect a system as has ever been realised in videogames. A single stick (the banana in the arcade machine, the GameCube analogue stick for most people) tilts the maze and causes the monkey to roll in the direction you're pushing. It is soft, responsive and unfailing, absolutely crucial for a skill test of this nature. Just as crucial is the camera, so often the ruin of platform games, but that, too, is handled elegantly. It follows your ball with intelligence and grace, and you will learn to direct it with gentle, subtle flicks of the control stick.

The mazes are increasingly complex in layout, but never to the point of becoming unfair. Beginning as straight, comforting, wonderfully solid plains to the goal, they soon narrow into worrying ledges and terrifying curves. Every single level feels like a real object in 3D space to conquer, and although there are often tricky shortcuts that will cut down your time and increase your score, there are never out-and-out tricks where

Play it now!

Since *Monkey Ball*'s GameCube debut the game has also been released on Xbox and PS2, but while these are competent enough conversions you're still better off seeking out the GameCube original thanks to the supreme suitability of the controller. The most recent version, for the Nintendo DS, is best forgotten.

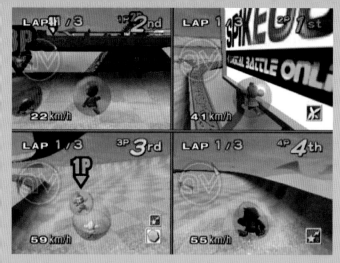

trial and error detective work is necessary to reach the goal. The sequel introduced that kind of gimmick to the game's detriment, but *Super Monkey Ball* is resolutely pure in concept and execution.

These lucid, beautiful structures are psychological hurdles as much as they are physical ones. Like the fairground puzzle where you trace a loop around an electric wire, making it to the end requires confidence as much as skill. If you start to worry too much about not being able to complete a level there's little chance you'll succeed, nervous hands dithering around needle-thin curves. But knowing that you *can* do a

level is half the battle. When a maze falls in *Monkey Ball* it falls forever in your head; you know you can do it now, and next time you try you'll wonder what the problem you ever had doing it before was. The difficulty spikes only serve to hammer that point home. The fifteenth level of the advanced set, the seventh level on expert difficulty; they seem impossible at first. Soon they're every bit as achievable as the levels before and after them.

The 'If at first you don't succeed' approach that *Super Monkey Ball* sometimes requires can be draining, and sometimes it's useful to step back for a little while and attempt something else. In these circumstances any minigames that could be unlocked and provide a diversion would become a Godsend. That many of the ones across all the versions of *Monkey Ball* rival the main game for invention and joy is testament to just how great they are. *Monkey Bowling* remains one of the most satisfying party games every devised, a simple ten pin bowl-

ing simulator accessible to everyone. *Monkey Flight* is more complex but graceful and addictive, *Monkey Fight* stupid and entertaining. Later titles include *Monkey Tennis*, *Monkey Boat*, and the phenomenal *Monkey Baseball*.

But after catching your breath you'll go back to the main game, relaxed and ready for another shot at whatever course was close to breaking you. Perhaps this time it'll fall, perhaps not; there's no denying that *Super Monkey Ball* is frustrating at times, but the rules never change and the frustration is always self-imposed. That's the element that makes it addictive. It's *always* your fault. You want to see what's next, to push on to the next challenge, and when there are no more challenges left there's an inner drive to go back and to them all over again; faster, better, smoother, stronger, to become the best guider of encapsulated monkeys in the whole goddamn universe.

Because *Monkey Ball* never loses its sense of humour, either. It's a self-aware videogame, never trying to be anything more than it is. So many games try to do so much and fail. This one concentrates on one, simple thing – the art of rolling – and does it so brilliantly it doesn't need to do anything else, offering challenge and satisfaction in every instant. So on top of everything else it teaches you something about game design. And, believe it or not, that something is not that banana-shaped controllers are a brilliant idea.

Tetris™

Publisher: Nintendo/various
Developer: Alexei Pajitnov
Platform: GameBoy, various
Released: 1985

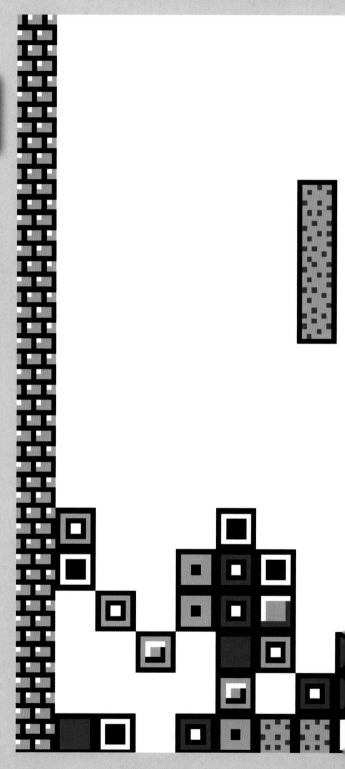

I f ever there was a game that needed no introduction, surely *Tetris* is it. Is there any other game that has been more talked about, or more written about or more analysed? Is there a game responsible for more sleepless nights? Is there, indeed, a game that's been played by more people, or for more hours than *Tetris*? This obviously presents a bit of a problem for anyone about to embark on a brief history of its brilliance: what is there left to say about the game that launched a hundred million handhelds? Not much, perhaps, but maybe it's still worth recapping, about its Russian creator; about the unseemly squabble for publishing rights; about its still unparalleled ubiquity. And maybe it's just worth reminding yourself about those hypnotic falling blocks that urge you to have just. one. more. go.

The game is as simple to describe as it is to play. Create horizontal lines by rotating and aligning geometrically shaped blocks that fall from the top of the screen. Fail to create enough lines and the playing field will start to fill up. When it's full, it's game over. That's it, in a nutshell. Simple. Except the game has now infected your brain and will continue in your head, with the blocks racing down the insides of your eyelids and the game's catchy theme tune continuing to reverberate inside your mind.

The game features seven different shapes, which roughly correspond in outline to the letters I, T, O, L, J, S, and Z, and the playing field is 10 blocks wide by 20 blocks high. Unbroken horizontal lines disappear when they are formed, leaving the blocks above them to shift downwards (though not quite according to gravity: they don't fall down to fill any gaps). Players receive extra points for clearing more than one line at the same time, and the speed with which the blocks descend increases over time – every ten lines the speed and scoring rate increases. Additional play modes start with the playing field already partly full for more of a challenge. And if you perform well you'll get to see a little animation depicting a rocket or space shuttle taking off while surrounded by little Russian dancers. And it's enormously addictive.

Its infectious appeal was clear from the outset. Its creator, Alexei Pajitnov struggled to finish programming the game because he was too busy playing it, and his colleagues were similarly transfixed when they were introduced to it. At the time, in 1984, he was working on AI systems at the Moscow Academy of Science, but inspired by a geometric puzzle called Pentominoes, he started prototyping his game on an Elektronika 60 (probably not even as powerful as modern day pocket calculators) before converting it to the only IBM PC in the building with the assistance of a schoolboy called Vadim Gerasimov. It wasn't long before Moscow businesses were forced to install a program that deleted the game as soon as it was run – in a bid to minimise its negative effect on the productivity of their workforce.

This unlikely origin prompted an equally unlikely, and unseemly, squabble for the game's global publishing rights. Although Pajitnov had created the game, the rights to publish it were held by the Russian State, who entered into negotiations with several bidders. Indeed at one point, three different bidders were negotiating with the Russians on the same day in the same building. One of these publishers happened to be a Japanese company who wanted the game for its new handheld console: the Game Boy. They got it. (As a footnote to Nintendo's success, the other two parties were: Robert Stein, a UK software agent who walked away with the arcade rights and home console versions; and Kevin Maxwell, negotiating on behalf of UK publisher Mirrosoft, who walked away empty-handed – prompting showdown talks between his media magnate father, Robert Maxwell, and Mikhail Gorbachev, then leader of the Soviet Union.)

Nintendo's interest had been piqued when Nintendo of America's president, Minorou Arakawa, had spotted it at a trade show in 1988 – a chance encounter that was to have far-reaching consequences. It's difficult to think of a game better suited to its host platform than Tetris was to the Game Boy. Available from the launch of the console, the game formed a cornerstone of the console's success. Given the game's simplicity, it was entirely untrammelled by the limitations of the device's limited colour palette, or 2.6-inch screen, and , fortuitously, the game proved perfectly portable: ideal for short playing sessions, but equally suited to zoned-out commuting spaces.

But while the Game Boy might have hastened the dissemination of the game, it wasn't entirely responsible for its success: the game (or one of its many imitators) is available on just about every electronic gaming platform, from consoles and home computers to mobile phones and PDAs. Most recently it has appeared on Nintendo's DS and Microsoft's Xbox 360, among others, and it remains the byword for both casual gaming and commercial success. But while many have tried, no other developer has ever matched the beguiling, elegant, purity of the game. Even Pajitnov himself has been unable to replicate the success of Tetris – though the absorbing puzzle game Hexic HD (which comes preinstalled on Xbox 360 Premium units) suggests that he hasn't given up trying.

Play it now!

It would take too much space to list the about-a-million versions of Tetris available for just about every different platform in existence today. Perhaps it will suffice to point out that the game continues to be ported to the most cutting-edge platforms, including the Nintendo DS (Tetris DS) and the Xbox 360 (Tetris: The Grandmaster Ace). It also continues to inspire new variations and imitations, including Tetsuya Mizuguchi's sublime Lumines, available for the PSP™.

Tomb Raider

Publisher: Eidos
Developer: Core Design Ltd
Platform: Saturn, PlayStation®, PC
Released: 1996

Lara through the ages. Different outfits, explosive adventures, same girl.

As far as the games industry goes, there's no one bigger than Lara Croft – and that's despite the fact her front proportions were reduced for her latest adventure *Tomb Raider: Legend*. From her humble beginnings on the Sega Saturn console to a true cyber celebrity able to draw news paparazzi when her real-life alter-ego hosts a photo-call, she's been *the* gaming icon for close to three generations of hardware.

This female figurehead for videogames the world over originated in Derby, England. Pre-production began in 1993, a world far removed from the one into which she emerged, blinking and pouting, three years later. Back in 1996, there was a cultural revolution as much as a gaming one. Girl Power met PlayStation® power at a pivotal moment, as the Spice Girls changed the social landscape, and Lara modelled a fresh gaming one.

As such, Lara's success cannot be attributed to any one person, or any one decision. She was the right person, in the right place, at right time. An accidental hero hanging on to the coat-tails of a manufactured pop act.

It could have been so much different: Lara was originally meant to be a man. Until quite late in the development process, this 3D action adventure boasted a facsimile Indiana Jones character, all rugged and

Her popularity with a mainstream audience changed the landscape of gaming forever

GAME ON

masculine. Quite rightly, developer Core Design decided that as the largest group of gamers at the time was male, most of them would prefer looking at an Indiana Jane, so to speak.

Of course, it's the anecdotal accidental slip of a mouse which also gave Lara Croft such an obvious visual impact. Creator Toby Gard was reportedly playing round with her dimensions in a wire-frame model when he moved one slidebar too far. In the flick of a hand, Lara's assets increased exponentially – but the team gathered round and decided they should go with the new model. Gard's boob produced, well, a distinctive pair of boobs – and Lara Croft as we have come to recognise her was born.

The original *Tomb Raider: Starring Lara Croft* – to give it its full title – saw Lara venturing into deepest Peru in order to retrieve a mysterious artefact on behalf of a conniving businesswoman. All relatively easy… or so it seems. However, the adventure soon takes a turn for the more dangerous, as Ms Croft realises it's a set up. What should have been a relatively simple expedition soon became a heart-stopping journey to

Europe, Egypt and, finally, Atlantis, as our buxom adventuress uncovered a mystery which has existed since the dawn of time itself. For a finale, she saved the world. And all without a hair out of place.

It was a proposition which captivated all who played. The awe of discovering a new location rendered in unprecedented 3D glory evoked memories of childhood exploration.

Stunning vistas coupled with crumbling, impressive structures made an awesome playground for gamers and their new female best friend. Illustrating a phenomenal capacity for genuine heart-in-mouth acrobatics, Lara danced majestically throughout the game's intricately designed levels. She explored jaw-dropping ruins, displaying incredible acrobatics skills. Who'd have though archaeology could have been so much fun?

To this day, *Tomb Raider* remains a genre-defining game. It wasn't perfect, however. Whilst Mario's move into three dimensions a few months prior had been largely trouble free, Core Design didn't boast the same expertise. Where Mario

64 was free-form and flowing, *Tomb Raider*'s grid-based level design required an awkward control movement. More often than not, it was the player's failure to grasp the mechanics of the staccato control method than a specific in-game threat which resulted in Lara's premature death.

But it's a testament to the overall package that such potentially game-breaking inadequacies are so easily overlooked. *Tomb Raider* was so much greater than the sum of its parts, and a landmark in interactive entertainment.

Tomb Raider II followed a year later, replacing the original's clever checkpoint system with the option to quick-save. This, sadly, also resulted in the introduction of instant death sequences. Where once players could feel free to explore, they now found themselves saving every few paces, interrupting the flow of the game.

Tomb Raider III followed 12 months after, and the incorrectly named *Tomb Raider The Last Revelation* a year after that. By then, the series was becoming gaming by numbers. Even Lara's death at the end of the fourth game didn't stop Eidos from continuing to milk the cash teats, with *Tomb Raider Chronicles* appearing, yes, the year after in 2000. Most memorably (for all the wrong reasons) the ill-fated *Angel Of Darkness* – perhaps the series' lowest point – arrived in 2003, after a troubled development period. It was a sham.

If Lara was a real woman, she'd have been checking into booze clinics and disgracing herself on chat-shows. But this is no ordinary female, and, following some tough decisions during the *Angel of Darkness* post-mortem, publisher Eidos shifted development from the UK to Crystal Dynamics in the United States. The firm even tempted back Lara Croft creator Toby Gard who left Core Design after the first game. As such, the latest release, *Tomb Raider: Legend* (PlayStation® 2, Xbox Xbox 360, PC, PSP™, 2006), is a genuine return to form.

Lara has come home. And a good job,

too. She is too big, too popular and too important to be left in the gutter. Her achievements include two successful films, a memorable appearance on the cover of *The Face* magazine and an entry in the *Guinness Book of Records* as 'The Most Successful Human Videogame Heroine'. She even appeared on stage with Bono during U2's Zooropa tour in the nineties.

Her success and, in particular, popularity with a mainstream audience changed the landscape of gaming forever, as well as the overall proportions of female videogame characters from then on. Long may her reign continue.

Play it now!

The original *Tomb Raider* doesn't quite have the same impact these days, but it's worth checking out in order to witness the origins of Lara. PC and PlayStation® versions remain widely available, and for a bargainous price, too. Several compilation packs are also on sale, offering multiple games in the series – though, as mentioned, the series does take a dive towards the latter stages. *Tomb Raider: Legend* is a return to form and absolutely worth a punt – particularly as Lara herself has never looked better.

Sometimes Lara wished she was 'Tropical Beach Raider'

Tony Hawk's Pro Skater 3

Publisher: Activision
Developer: Neversoft Entertainment
Platform: PlayStation® 2
Released: 2001

Sometimes it's advancing technology that brings new opportunities to gaming, refreshing old genres and giving rise to new ones. Faster processors and better graphics chips mean that developers can suddenly do justice to concepts they've struggled to bring to life for many years. But as much as technological changes are important in birthing new ideas, so are cultural ones. Whatever's in vogue is what people want, and that makes successful game development not just about coming up with that breakthrough idea, but coming up with the right idea at the right time. Enter *Tony Hawk's Pro Skater*, Neversoft's perfectly pitched skate series.

There are three main reasons why its game conquered all. First up: technology. The genesis of affordable 3D gaming hardware in the shape of the Nintendo64 and Sony's PlayStation® meant that all of a sudden the slopes and pipes of the perfect skate park, the concrete angles and metal railings of electronic skaters' dreams could be made solid and workable in digital fiction. Environments that were only possible side-on in pixels before could be rendered as real, and a sport that had been limited to two dimensions gained new weight in three.

Second, culture. The PlayStation® brought a new audience and a new edge to gaming, a hypercool bracket of brand-conscious teens and twenty-somethings whose gaming purchases had to be in sync with their lifestyles. Looking for something as cool as every other aspect of their delicately selected lives, they found skateboarding. Skating was, is, and always will be cool. If Neversoft could impart that their game was part of that aggressively hip niche they'd have little problem selling it. Hence the Tony Hawk branding, the game taking the

SCORE: 3750

CASH 25
GOAL PTS. 0

BS 5-0 + BS CROOKED
1215 X 2

2940 X 1
BS Boneless

SCORE: 219

CASH 0
GOAL PTS. 0

7800 X 1
The 900

Hold on, that's a GIRL. I thought this game was meant to be realistic

BS BLUNTSLIDE
1270

DAPPY CHEF

WASSUP?!

EXIT

YOUR DADDY!

CAUTION

PROPS. DUDE

BS FEEBLE
2165

SCORE: 420

CASH 0
GOAL PTS. 0

BS NOSESLIDE

350 X 1
Crossbone

SCORE 567
SPECIAL

SWITCH

360 ROASTBEEF

SCORE 2220
SPECIAL

HARDFLIP
300

SCORE: 0

CASH
GOAL PTS.

115

360 JUDO
3000

965 X 2
BS Smith + BS Bluntslide

Is 'manual' skater-speak for 'fall flat on your arse'?

BONELESS + OLLIE NORTH

VARIAL HEELFLIP

name of skating's number one superstar. *Tony Hawk's Pro Skater* was real, authentic and impeccably timed.

It's the third reason that's perhaps the most important. Neversoft could have taken several different gaming's genres as the base for their title, but they didn't play skateboarding as if it were a race, or overcomplicate the simulation aspect. They produced what amounts to a quick, slick platform game on four wheels. Each of the first three games in the series takes place in a series of skate parks, mostly disguised as real world locations. The player rides around these locales performing tricks and earning points, trying to better their previous score with increasingly spectacular stunts.

But the challenge in *Tony Hawk's Pro Skater* – and the reason the game is most like a platform game – isn't in learning the controls so much as learning the environments and how to negotiate them. Each of the rich, character-filled arenas hides a number of secrets and special areas. Working out how to get to them using tricks and your skater's momentum is a great part of the game's appeal. There's a huge sense of achievement when you trick your way up a series of railings and kick flip into a new part of the level, the same sort of feeling you'd get if you'd done it for real. We'd imagine.

Each of the levels has a number of different challenges to encourage you to explore the environment, and though completing each of these has a compulsive charm, it's the straight out high-score attacks that force you to master Tony Hawk's tricking system. If the main game is a platform game

then the tricks are taken direct from a beat-'em-up, letting you link sharp, fast special moves together into rewarding, high-scoring combos. But the truth is that there's so much fun in just skating around the world that even those who can't get to grips with complex mid-air dynamics will enjoy themselves. Hitting X makes your skater jump, momentum will be your instinctive friend on the half-pipe, and the dirty, bone-shuddering impact as he makes an awkward landing face-first will do wonders for persuading you to time your aerial movements better next time.

And persevere you will, just like millions before you. Easy to get into, hard to leave alone, and effortlessly cool, *Tony Hawk's* is one of a select band of games that has had as much of a cultural effect on the world around it as the world did on the game. Neversoft can be proud of itself; it's at least partially responsible for the modern uptake in skateboarding amongst teenagers, and it's certainly made Tony Hawk into a household name. More than that, it's created a fun, unique franchise that doesn't just appeal to people who like the concept of defying gravity on a board. Right place at the right time, maybe, but you still need people who have the right idea to make it all work.

Play it now!

Modern versions of the *Tony Hawk's Pro Skater* series have been differently branded: *Tony Hawk's Underground 1&2*, or *Tony Hawk's American Wasteland*. They continue to have the same free roaming, tricking appeal, but the RPG element that first appeared in *Tony Hawk's Pro Skater 4* has spoilt the game for many who regard *Tony Hawk's Pro Skater 3* as the pinnacle of the franchise.

Tony Hawk's Pro Skater 3 © 2001 Activision Publishing Inc.

Virtua Tennis

Publisher:	Sega
Developer:	Sega
Platform:	Arcade, DC
Released:	1999

Every once in a while a game comes to the arcade that makes people take a step back and realise just how far gaming has come in such a short space of time. *Virtua Tennis* doesn't look too bad today, but when it came out right at the start of the 21st century it looked absolutely beautiful. The character models were so detailed and moved so well, so realistically, so much better than any of its rivals. They were modelled on real-life tennis players and if you squinted you could almost think you were watching footage beamed live from a Grand Slam.

The thing is, once you've stripped away the gorgeous visuals there really isn't much to *Virtua Tennis*. Which is somewhat of a tradition in gobsmacking arcade games -- remember *Dragon's Lair*, the video CD 'interactive cartoon'? -- but is also fine, because if you think about it there isn't much in any tennis game that wasn't in the original *Pong*, one of the only video games that's the wrong side of thirty. There is a bat and there is a ball, and the objective is to keep the ball from passing the bat. What more is there to tennis?

So it follows that *Virtua Tennis* gives you control of a (somewhat photorealistic, at least for the era) tennis player on one side of a court, facing another tennis player on the other side of a net. Those are the digital bats, and soon the digital ball starts to move between them, picking up pace as it crosses the net. You move into position with the arcade stick and in order to hit the ball you can use one of two buttons, stroke and lob. Once you've pressed the button your player stops running and while they're anticipating the arrival of the ball you have an opportunity to direct it in whatever direction you choose, striking it to the part of the court your opponent will find the most difficult to reach.

Two buttons and a joystick. In the face of control systems for sports games that were gettting ever more complicated, *Virtua Tennis'* simplified approach was a revelation. There were no complicated button sequences to remember, no special moves or secret joystick techniques. This was a method of control that anyone could remember, a game setup that anyone could involve themselves immediately. It might be an order of magnitude more complex than *Pong*, but that still holds today, of course.

Which is useful because, perhaps predictably, one of *Virtua Tennis'* greatest strengths is in multiplayer. Since the game's ruleset is so simple to learn there's very little time when one player knows a great deal more about the way the game works than the other, the sort of thing that makes multiplayer gaming so harsh on newcomers. Games come down to precision, quick thinking, skill and a little bit of luck. *Virtua Tennis* is a perfect party game, offering the same sort of appeal as mashing buttons in *SoulCalibur*. It's easy to start and it's easy to get good. It's hard to get brilliant, but that's what practice is for.

FUJIFILM
evian

15 - 0

COM   0
1P   15

1 P   Pioline
COM   Henman
Games
NORMAL

COM   Johansson
COM   Haas
Games

COM COM   0
1P   COM   0

0 km/h

BRIDGESTONE   U.S. SUPER TENNIS   BRIDGESTONE   Wweid
COM   Pioline
2 P   Haas
Games
NORMAL

COM   Moya
COM   Philippoussis
Games

COM COM   0
COM 2P   0

RESULTS

SPT TOUR

IP VS. COM

Henman   Pioline

1 Game   0 Game

play time   0min 49sec
0   service aces   0
0   smash points   0
3   points at the net   0
PRIZE MONEY $0
TOTAL $643.905

COM   Pioline

Balle de match
40 - 15

COM 1 5
● 1P 40

For those who'd rather play it alone than with friends, the Dreamcast version of the game offers a comprehensive array of solitary entertainment. An arcade mode mirrors the quick fix on offer in the arcade version, allowing you to select one of the eight licensed characters and take them through five short matches. Exhibition mode gives you the chance to set up a practice match, single or doubles; it's another opportunity to get a quick fix of *Virtua Tennis*'s addictive, simplistic gameplay.

The main addition for the home version is the World Circuit mode in which you embark on a quest to become the number one tennis player in the world. For better or worse it's not a traditional videogame quest, the sort that involves slaying goblins and exchanging lightning bolts with wizards in towers. It's one where you have to play other people at tennis, filling in the time between tournaments with a series of diverting (if slightly outlandish) training games. In those you have to return the ball at boxes, or tin cans, or other targets. To be honest it's not that much different from hitting the ball back at an opponent.

That's fine, because it's the hitting the ball part that's fun. *Virtua Tennis* is a perfect working example of how sometimes the best thing gaming can do is keep it simple. That doesn't mean you can't have beauty, power or subtlety of control. It just means that everyone can enjoy it. And what's not to enjoy about *Pong*?

Play it now!

The definitive conversion of the original *Virtua Tennis* is the Dreamcast version, but as Sega's machine is long since gone you'd be better off sticking with the latest PSP™ version. Released in 2005, *Virtua Tennis World Tour* is easy to come by and offers all the addictive simplicity of the original, along with new modes and new characters.

Tim hoped no-one would spot his secret weapon

Wario Ware™
Inc.: Minigame Mania

Publisher: Nintendo
Developer: Nintendo
Platform: GameBoy Advance
Released: 2003

Each microgame concludes with a pass or fail for the player. Four fails and the medley ends. Keep succeeding and the game plays out faster and faster until the challenges become a fast-forward blur of graphics and a glitchy twitch of sound. Eventually, inevitably, you fail, and the game cackles at you, records your score and invites you to play again.

Perhaps it's important to distinguish between these micro-games and the minigames that are often offered as bonuses in other titles. *Wario Ware*'s microgames are truly microscopic, not just in terms of the fraction of a time they take from beginning to end, but also in the scope for interaction that they offer the player. This is reductive gaming at its finest: many of the set-pieces use one button alone, and you get the feeling that if it were possible to have a game where no buttons were used the *Wario Ware* developers would jump at the chance to do so. Indeed, they moved a step closer to that in the sequel, *Wario Ware Twisted*, which used a motion-sensing cartridge to minimise the button pressing still further.

It's also important to understand just how much *Wario Ware*'s various settings and visual aspect fits the title. This isn't a game with a coherent vision, or if it is then the vision is to have no vision. It's like a game that got dressed by stumbling through twenty different ward-robes, emerging blinking and grinning to your disapproving gaze. One game you have to pick your nose. In one you have to catch apples thrown by a monkey. Another sees you tipping a ball left and right through a maze. One gets you recognising fruit through a small slit in

Answering basic questions about *Wario Ware* turns out to be more difficult than you'd imagine. What sort of game is *Wario Ware*? Well, it's sort of like no particular genre, really, or you could say it's like them all, a tiny bit of everything mashed up with everything else. Ok then, what does *Wario Ware* look like? Hmm. It looks like … lots of different things. Like a kid's drawing and photorealistic montage and cartoon and abstract art and Manga and eight-bit videogames and Mr Potato Head. What does it play like? It plays like nothing else on Earth, obviously.

As always it's best to start at the beginning. *Wario Ware* is a collection of dozens and dozens of microgames, each a handful of seconds long. In the standard single-player mode the game throws a non-stop medley of these at you. Which is to say that when one microgame finishes *Wario Ware* segues immediately into the next. The next almost certainly bears very little relation to the last, visually or physically, and then it's over almost as soon as it has begun and you move on again.

244

a wall. There is a game in which you control a ski jumper's precise point of lift off, and another where you shake hands with a dog. Eat hotdogs, guide jugglers, dress Wario, and so on through a hundred more.

There is no stylistic thread running through all these tasks. Some look like they're working with test graphics, wobbly lines in monochrome, while others have rich textures and characters that feel like they've been stolen from something larger. In some cases they have -- there's a series of challenges in which you guide classic Nintendo characters through microcosms of their own games. Jump on someone's head in *Mario*, enter a cave in *Zelda*, avoid crashing in *F-Zero*. Each cycles in, spends five seconds at the front of your mind, and then vanishes again.

Even the bigger 'mini' games, which provide a change of pace from the frantic nature of the medley centrepiece, are largely triumphs of design over content. In *Paper Plane* you can steer clockwise and anticlockwise to weave a paper plane through a series of obstacles. In *Skipping Rope* you hit a button to jump over a skipping rope, again and again and again. In *Fly Swatter* you swat flies, in *Puro* and *Puro 2* you use your tongue to …

… Well, you get the idea. There is so much to do in *Wario Ware*, and though all of those things are tiny tasks, the game somehow becomes far more than the sum of its parts. Perhaps that's why it's so difficult to describe, because in listing all the elements you leave out the whole, the way they all fit together to make something so full of joy. For all its retro stylings, *Wario Ware* felt like a breath of fresh air when it first appeared in 2003, and it's still an improbable amount of fun today.

Play it now!

Wario Ware has spawned a couple of sequels: *Wario Ware Twisted* contains a tilt sensor which means you have to tilt the machine to win some of the games, while *Wario Ware: Touch!* is the DS version which uses both the stylus and the microphone. Both are fun, but neither are as good as the addictive original, which is increasingly difficult to find. As always, second-hand games stores or eBay will help.

Wario Ware™ Inc.: Minigame Mania EU © 2003 Nintendo.

World of Warcraft

Publisher: Vivendi Universal Games
Developer: Blizzard Entertainment
Platform: PC
Released: 2004

Dungeons! Dragons! Swords! Sorcery! All traditional ports of call for the veteran videogame fan, but *World of Warcraft* does the adventuring differently. Sure, you're still slaying, still questing, still seeking peril in a beautiful, bewitching land – but this time you're playing with thousands of other real people, all online in the same universe at the same time, all seeking fame and fortune in the same place you are.

Not that role playing with friends is a new thing. Some thirty years ago, tabletop gaming with the original *Dungeons & Dragons* fostered the teenage love of gaming with pen-and-paper swords and sorcery. Videogames stole the setting for text-based games called Multi-User Dungeons, digital facsimiles that removed the dice rolling and replaced human game masters with computer ones. These static, stats-based adventures ultimately evolved into the lusciously depicted, collaborative graphical realms of today; alternate realities where those who wish to fight with magic or dress in chain mail can go and live their dreams. There is a phrase for these online places: they are called Massively Multiplayer Online Role Playing Games, or MMORPGs, and the best of

them all is *World of Warcraft. World of Warcraft* isn't so much a game as an international phenomenon.

Before you enter the world of Azeroth, you begin by choosing who you are: good or evil. Players across the world have to select from two factions – the Alliance and the Horde – and the races within them. The Alliance is the 'good' collection of races, humans, night elves, dwarves and gnomes, righteous chaps all, with hearts of gold and appearances to match.

Buffy

dClaw   Almendra   Johnathan Pride   Daltlynn   Brawnson

No-one could agree whose turn it
was to buy the big fella a drink

KOBOLD TUNNEL

This year Farmer Palmer wasn't taking any chances with crows

Studded leather and Ugg boots are the hot new look. Again.

The Horde is the traditionally evil side: Orcs, Tauren, the Undead and Trolls, significantly less attractive and consequently more intimidating. Already *World of Warcraft*'s age-old battle is set up, and already the player has chosen their future. All that is left to do now is to choose their class (from Druid, Hunter, Mage, Paladin, Priest, Rogue, Shaman, Warlock and Warrior, each of which gives different abilities) and begin an adventure that will never end.

That adventure may not look like a phenomenon at the start. Your player begins his or her epic quest alone as a low-level hero, hunting small things on easy quests, and few hints of the grandeur to come. This is no game of reactions; hunting things involves careful weapon selection, selecting your target with the mouse, and watching the result as a bank of computers at the other end of an internet connection do all the dice rolling for you. It hardly sounds thrilling, but this is *World of Warcraft*'s equivalent of a tutorial, and eventually you're encouraged to leave the beginner's area to find bigger quests – and to join in with others as they do the same.

In the wide world you'll meet other human players and journey with them, and soon you're part of a guild, slaying things co-operatively, fighting in the shadows of ten-foot beasts. But as big as the enemies get they can always get bigger, and as you click and kill bigger things, so you earn more

Once again the ability to light farts came in handy

taken by self-aware massively multiplayer players and used to define the point that repetitive mechanics for pointless rewards seem less like pleasure, more like work – but it's the community aspect that makes the grind not just palatable but insatiably addictive. *World of Warcraft* is a chatroom where everyone has something in common: that burning desire for in-game success, fame and fortune. And as you might expect with something heavily reliant on human interaction, the battleground becomes a soap opera. True friendships are formed, real-life rivalries developed. Social dramas unfold with regularity, just as often inspired by players' personalities as they are by Blizzard's smartly balanced mechanics.

Which is why it is a game of the moment, one as dependent on its community as its community is dependent on the developer providing new content. An expansion pack which raises the top level to seventy will be out shortly and new lands and new quests will keep the adventurers hooked. As long as Blizzard keeps entertaining its paying customers their attention is ensured, and as long as they're still there then Azeoroth will remain a rich, beautiful world that's as simple to enter as it is difficult to leave.

experience points. As you earn more experience points, so your level goes up. And as your level goes up, so you can kill bigger things, and this is that things continue until – hundreds of hours of playtime later, and tens of thousands of enemies vanquished – you hit level sixty, the current top level for all players. And that's it, right?

No. The draw is that the next level and new skills always seem just around the corner, just one more quest away; it is an insanely powerful, primal addiction, and reaching sixty might be a relief for those who have lost themselves in Azeroth. But there is no end-game, no finality in an MMORPG. These are online games, constantly updated, and that means the developer can constantly provide new challenges for their players, new quests to feed their subscribers' thirst for more.

Just as the game world is constantly evolving, so are the objectives of high level players. Reached the top at level sixty? Now you'll crave the perfect weapon, the prettiest armour sets. You and your battle-scarred party will embark on more epic quests against ludicrously powerful monsters. When that quest is over the final monster may, if you're lucky, drop a rare item. If you're unlucky then you'll just do the quest over and over until they *get* lucky, and receive the reward of that sought-after trinket. And there are always more trinkets to find; brighter armour, better weapons…

It sounds like a grind. In some respects it is a grind – a term

Play it now!

World of Warcraft isn't difficult to get hold of, nor particularly expensive – but buyers should be aware that, at the time of writing, it requires a subscription fee of just under nine pounds a month. Premium expansion packs will also cost money; an MMORPG habit can be quite costly if you're intending to keep up with your fellow clanmembers.

Permissions

The publisher and authors would like to thank the following for giving permission to reproduce copyright material:

Advance Wars™: Dual Strike
© 2005 Nintendo / INTELLIGENT SYSTEMS.

Animal Crossing™: Wild World
© 2005 Nintendo.

Asteroids
© 2006 Atari Interactive Inc. All Rights Reserved. Asteroids is a registered trademark of Atari Interactive Inc.

Bangai-O (US, Europe)
N64/JP © TREASURE/ESP 1999
DC/JP © TREASURE/ESP 1999
DC/EU © 2000 TREASURE/ESP. Translation © 2000 Swing!
DC/US © 2001 TREASURE/ESP. Translation © 2001 Conspiracy.

Battlefield 1942™
© 2002 Digital Illusions CE AB. All rights reserved. Battlefield 1942 is a trademark of Digital Illusions CE AB. Electronic Arts, EA GAMES and the EA GAMES logo are trademarks or registered trademarks of Electronic Arts Inc. in the U.S. and/or other countries. EA GAMES™ is an Electronic Arts™ brand.

Broken Sword: The Shadow of the Templars
© 1996 Revolution Software Ltd.;
Broken Sword II The Smoking Mirror © 1997 Revolution Software Ltd.;
Broken Sword The Sleeping Dragon © 2003 Revolution Software Ltd.

Call of Duty 2
© 2005 Activision Publishing, Inc.

Command & Conquer™
ELECTRONIC ARTS, EA, EA SPORTS, EA SPORTS BIG, EA GAMES, EA STORE, ORIGIN, BULLFROG, MAXIS, WESTWOOD STUDIOS, POGO, CLUB POGO, POGO.COM, all associated logos and 'Challenge Everything' are trademarks, registered trademarks or service marks of Electronic Arts Inc. in the U.S. and/or other countries.

EA™, EA GAMES™, EA SPORTS™, EA SPORTS BIG™, Pogo™, ORIGIN™, Bullfrog™, Maxis™ and Westwood Studios™ are Electronic Arts™ brands.
Compilation © 2006 Electronic Arts Inc. Electronic Arts, EA, EA logo, Command and Conquer, Command and Conquer The Covert Operation, Command and Conquer Red Alert, The Aftermath, Command and Conquer Red Alert Counterstrike, Tiberian Sun, Firestorm, Command and Conquer Renegade and Yuri's Revenge are trademarks or registered trademarks of Electronic Arts Inc. in the U.S. and/or other countries. All Rights Reserved. All other trademarks are the property of their respective oweners. EA™ is an Electronic Arts™ brand.

Dance Dance Revolution
© Konami Corporation. All Rights Reserved.

Dead or Alive 4
Microsoft product screen shot(s) reprinted with permission from Microsoft Corporation.

The Elder Scrolls® IV: Oblivion™
 © 2006 Bethesda Softworks LLC, a ZeniMax Media company. The Elder Scrolls, Oblivion, Bethesda Game Studios, Bethesda Softworks, ZeniMax and related logos are registered trademarks or trademarks of ZeniMax Media Inc. in the U.S. and/or other countries. 2K Games and the 2K Games logo are registered trademarks or trademarks of Take-Two Interactive Software.
Microsoft, Xbox, Xbox 360, Xbox Live, and the Xbox, Xbox 360, and Xbox Live logos are either registered trademarks or trademarks of Microsoft Corporation in the U.S. and/or other countries.

Elite
© Bell & Braben 1984.

EyeToy®: Play
© 2003 Sony Computer Entertainment Europe. Developed by London Studio. Published by Sony Computer Entertainment Europe. EyeToy and EyeToy: Play are trademarks of Sony Computer Entertainment Europe. All Rights Reserved.

FINAL FANTASY VII
©1997 SQUARE ENIX CO., LTD. All Rights Reserved.
FINAL FANTASY is a registered trademark of Square Enix Co., Ltd.
CHARACTER DESIGN :TETSUYA NOMURA.

F-Zero™ GX
© 2003 Nintendo. © AMUSEMENT VISION / SEGA, 2003.

Golden Eye 007™
©1997 Nintendo/Rare. Game by Rare. © 1962, 1995 Danjaq, LLC. & U.A.C. All Rights Reserved. © 1997 Eon Productions Ltd/ & Mac B Inc. James Bond theme by Monty Norman. Used by permission of EMI Unart Inc.

Grand Theft Auto III
© 2001 Rockstar Games. All Rights Reserved.

Gran Turismo 4
© 2004 Sony Computer Entertainment Inc.
All manufacturers, cars, names, brands and associated imagery featured in this game are trademarks and/or copyrighted materials of their respective owners. All rights reserved. Any depiction or recreation of real world locations, entities, businesses, or organizations is not intended to be or imply any sponsorship or endorsement of this game by such party or parties.

Guitar Hero
RedOctane® is a registered trademark of RedOctane, Inc. Guitar Hero is a trademark of RedOctane, Inc. Developed by Harmonix Music Systems. ©2005-2006 RedOctane, Inc. All Rights Reserved.

Half-Life
Thanks to Valve LLC and Havas Interactive.

Halo: Combat Evolved
Reprinted with permission from Microsoft Corporation.

Ico™
© 2001 Sony Computer Entertainment Inc.

Jak and Daxter: The Precursor Legacy™
© 2001 Sony Computer Entertainment Inc.

Jet Set Radio Future
© SEGA. All Rights Reserved.

The Legend of Zelda™: Ocarina of Time™
© 1998 Nintendo.

Lumines
© 2005 Q ENTERTAINMENT and Bandai Program © 2005 Q ENTERTAINMENT and Bandai. Published and distributed by Ubisoft Entertainment. Ubisoft and the Ubisoft logo are trademarks of Ubisoft Entertainment in the U.S. and/or other countries. LUMINES is a trademark of Bandai. All Rights Reserved.

Madden NFL 06
© 2005 Electronic Arts Inc. Electronic Arts, EA, EA SPORTS and the EA SPORTS logo are trademarks or registered trademarks of Electronic Arts Inc. in the U.S. and/or other countries. All rights reserved. The mark 'John Madden' and the name, likeness and other attributes of John Madden reproduced on this product are trademarks or other intellectual property of Red Bear, Inc. or John Madden, are subject to license to Electronic Arts Inc., and may not be otherwise used in whole or in part without the prior written consent of Red Bear or John Madden. © 2005 NFL Properties LLC. Team names/logos are trademarks of the teams indicated. All other NFL-related trademarks are trademarks of the National Football League. Officially licensed product of PLAYERS INC. THE PLAYERS INC logo is a registered trademark of the NFL players. www.nflplayers.com © 2005 PLAYERS INC. Riddell is a registered trademark of Ridmark Corporation. All other trademarks are the property of their respective owners. EA SPORTS™ is an Electronic Arts™ brand.

Mario Kart™ DS
© 2005 Nintendo

Metal Gear Solid
© Konami Corporation. All Rights Reserved

OutRun
© SEGA. All Rights Reserved.

Pac-Man™
© NAMCO BANDAI Games Inc.

Pokémon™ Ruby/Sapphire
©2003 Pokemon. ©1995-2003 Nintendo/Creatures Inc./GAME FREAK Inc.

Pong
© 2006 Atari Interactive Inc. All Rights Reserved. Pong is a registered trademark of Atari Interactive Inc.

Pro Evolution Soccer 5
© Konami Corporation. All Rights Reserved.

Resident Evil™ 4
©CAPCOM CO., LTD. 2005 All Rights Reserved.

Rez
© 2001 Sony Computer Entertainment Inc.
All manufacturers, cars, names, brands and associated imagery featured in this game are trademarks and/or copyrighted materials of their respective owners. All rights reserved. Any depiction or recreation of real world locations, entities, businesses, or organizations is not intended to be or imply any sponsorship or endorsement of this game by such party or parties.

Acknowledgements

Simon Byron would like to thank Graeme Struthers, Tim Ponting, Jennie Kong, Doug Lombardi, CJ Gibson, Simon Smith-Wright, Shaun White, Dave Miller, Ed Valiente, Charles Cecil, Tomio Kanazawa, Martin Defries and, particularly, Alex Huhtala, without whom the 50 Best Games wouldn't have included perhaps the best game ever. Additionally, he would like to thank his friends and family, for their continued support and tolerance.

David McCarthy would like to thank Stefan McGarry, Rob Saunders, Jennie Kong, Hayley Shield, Carolina Pittol, Charlotte McConnell, Ian Bell, David Braben, Masato Maegawa, Shino Hori, James Beaven, Marie-Claire Suter, Shaun White, Simon Smith-Wright, Ed Valiente, Erica Bannerman, iainl, Derek from the Block, tingle, Gnoop, and, of course, his inspirational co-authors. And his family, obviously.

Ste Curran would like to thank Sam Brace, Adrian Lawton, Jamie Ingram, Manab Roy, Cat Channon, Simon Wells, Rob Saunders, Marie-Claire Suter, Stefan McGarry, Ed Daly, all of Kuju Brighton, and www.improperlanguage.com. He extends his undying gratitude to The Triforce, without whom this book would not exist, and its consistently amazing users. His friends and family are awesome, too.